SEARCHING
FOR THE
PHILOSOPHERS'
STONE

T0322888

"Ralph Metzner is a great storyteller! These life tales overflow with amazing events, profound insights, sorrowful traumas, and madcap adventures. We share the times, places, and teachers—human, plants, fungi, and animals—that expanded his worldview from the narrow rational/material to the spiritual and beyond to the shamanistic."

JAMES FADIMAN, PH.D., AUTHOR OF
THE PSYCHEDELIC EXPLORER'S GUIDE

"A biographical journey of self-awareness through deep meditations, mind-transforming substances, and the spiritual embrace of humans, animals, and dreams. I recommend this work for the seeker in all of us."

PETER PHILLIPS, PH.D., PROFESSOR OF POLITICAL SOCIOLOGY
AT SONOMA STATE UNIVERSITY AND
AUTHOR OF *GIANTS: THE GLOBAL POWER ELITE*

"From the 1960s to the present, Metzner has occupied a central role as an experimental scientist, educator, and healer, leaving no philosophers' stone unturned, mapping consciousness in both scholarly and personal ways in the enduring tradition of Jung and Campbell, Huxley and Watts."

MICHAEL HOROWITZ, COEDITOR OF
ALDOUS HUXLEY'S *MOKSHA* AND *SISTERS OF THE EXTREME*

"What a fascinating life Ralph Metzner has lived and what marvelous mentors he's had along the way! The stories in *Searching for the Philosophers' Stone* are filled with charm, wonder, surprise, warmth, and bold insights into consciousness. Metzner's diverse human guides are astute and compassionate. Just as impressive are the spirit world teachers, who speak by way of animals, dreams, meditative states, and, of course, mind-altering plants and other entheogens."

ALLEN D. KANNER, PH.D., COEDITOR OF *ECOPSYCHOLOGY* AND
PSYCHOLOGY AND CONSUMER CULTURE

"This beautiful chronicle of spiritual discovery, where each story is a jewel shining with truth and wisdom, documents a great and courageous journey into expanded consciousness."

MATTHEW MCKAY, PH.D., AUTHOR OF *SEEKING JORDAN*

"Few people have written as many life-changing books as Ralph Metzner, and nobody has written about profound topics more eloquently. *Searching for the Philosophers' Stone* is no exception, and his collection of conversations with remarkable men and women will give readers a glimpse of inner and outer worlds that they never knew existed."

STANLEY KRIPPNER, PH.D., COAUTHOR OF *PERSONAL MYTHOLOGY*

"Metzner beautifully fulfills his role as wisdom carrier with *Searching for the Philosophers' Stone*. His stories reveal an intuitive mind, an integrated psyche, and steadfast allegiance to his life mission: to cultivate approaches to healing our fractured psyches/bodies in this fractured world by drawing on time-honored mythology, expanded states of perception, and shamanistic practices of times past and present. The book is a tale of adventure well flavored by Metzner's curiosity and humility."

CHELLIS GLENDINNING, PH.D., PSYCHOLOGIST AND AUTHOR OF
*MY NAME IS CHELLIS AND I'M IN RECOVERY FROM
WESTERN CIVILIZATION* AND *THE HISTORY MAKERS*

"Part memoir, part vision quest, Metzner shares his moving experiences of fatherhood and loss; meetings with masters, both human and other worldly; dream state and power animal transmissions; and more. He earns his place as a chief influencer in today's positive resurgence of the psychedelic psychotherapy movement and also as a true scholar of human consciousness."

JAMY FAUST, M.A. & PETER FAUST, M.AC., COAUTHORS OF
*THE CONSTELLATION APPROACH: FINDING PEACE
THROUGH YOUR FAMILY LINEAGE*

"Ralph Metzner is a brilliant psychologist and writer whose stellar consciousness research helped to shape the path of an entire generation of spiritual seekers, including my own. This is an amazing treatise on the remarkable, wild, and profound life and teachings of Ralph that led to the development of his alchemical divination, which has touched the hearts of countless souls searching for the meaning of life. Through fascinating stories and his pioneering research he has opened us up to amazing wisdom and cosmologies from multiple dimensions."

SANDRA INGERMAN, M.A., COAUTHOR OF *SPEAKING WITH NATURE* AND AUTHOR OF *THE BOOK OF CEREMONY*

"This amazing autobiographical volume is overflowing with rare and unique information not found anywhere else. Beautifully recounting his transformative journey, with a global cast of notable mystics, scientists, and healers, Metzner describes how these encounters led him to insights that were far beyond what he was expecting."

DAVID JAY BROWN, AUTHOR OF *DREAMING WIDE AWAKE* AND *THE NEW SCIENCE OF PSYCHEDELICS*

"*Searching for the Philosophers' Stone* is a cause for celebration that takes us on an enlivening, robust, eye-opening journey with the people and practices that have shaped Metzner's thinking and vision of an awakened life. This personal account of his path as a legendary pioneer in the field of consciousness also reflects the broader history of this movement in America. This is a book that both skeptics and believers will find riveting and enlightening."

RICHARD STROZZI-HECKLER, AUTHOR OF *IN SEARCH OF THE WARRIOR SPIRIT* AND *THE LEADERSHIP DOJO*

"Ralph Metzner is one of the legendary visionary pioneers of today's consciousness movement. He records his experiences with both entheogens and mystical practices. This book provides psychological insights that are the result of many decades of deep inquiry. It is a treasure."

JEFFREY MISHLOVE, PH.D., HOST OF *NEW THINKING ALLOWED*

"As an educator there can be no greater journey of the self toward the Self. This book provides the catalyst one needs to explore the inner dimensions for coherence with our outer work."

PHILIP SNOW GANG, PH.D., ACADEMIC DEAN OF THE INSTITUTE FOR EDUCATIONAL STUDIES MASTER OF EDUCATION PROGRAMS AT ENDICOTT COLLEGE

SEARCHING
FOR THE
PHILOSOPHERS' STONE

Encounters with Mystics,
Scientists, and Healers

RALPH METZNER, PH.D.

Park Street Press
Rochester, Vermont

Park Street Press
One Park Street
Rochester, Vermont 05767
www.ParkStPress.com

Text stock is SFI certified

Park Street Press is a division of Inner Traditions International

Library of Congress Cataloging-in-Publication Data

Names: Metzner, Ralph, author.
Title: Searching for the philosophers' stone : encounters with mystics, scientists, and healers / Ralph Metzner.
Description: Rochester, Vermont : Park Street Press, 2018. | Includes bibliographical references and index.
Identifiers: LCCN 2018015923 (print) | LCCN 2018023132 (ebook) | ISBN 9781620557761 (paperback) | ISBN 9781620557778 (ebook)
Subjects: LCSH: Ayahuasca—Physiological effect. | Hallucinogenic Drugs—Psychological aspects. | Consciousness. | Psychotherapy. | BISAC: SOCIAL SCIENCE / Popular Culture. | BIOGRAPHY & AUTOBIOGRAPHY / Philosophers.
Classification: LCC BF209.A93 M47 2018 (print) | LCC BF209.A93 (ebook) | DDC 615.7/883—dc23
LC record available at https://lccn.loc.gov/2018015923

Printed and bound in the United States by Lake Book Manufacturing, Inc. The text stock is SFI certified. The Sustainable Forestry Initiative® program promotes sustainable forest management.

10 9 8 7 6 5 4 3 2 1

Text design and layout by Priscilla Baker
This book was typeset in Garamond Premier Pro with Posterama 1901, Myriad Pro, and Legacy Sans used as display typefaces

To send correspondence to the author of this book, mail a first-class letter to the author c/o Inner Traditions • Bear & Company, One Park Street, Rochester, VT 05767, and we will forward the communication, or contact the author directly at **www.greenearthfound.org**.

To my beloved daughter
Sophia Marija

———

I dedicate this book of stories to all who walk
on the pathways of inclusive wholeness—exploring and
cherishing the uniqueness of our human beingness, the
diversity of species and cultures on this magnificent
planet Earth, and the boundless grandeur of the
ever-expanding Universe.

CONTENTS

INTRODUCTION

MY QUEST FOR THE PHILOSOPHERS' STONE

Searching for the philosophers' stone (the *lapis philosophorum*) is the key central metaphor of the alchemical tradition, as the *journey* for healing and vision is the central metaphoric process in shamanism, and *liberation* from illusory attachments is the central preoccupation of yoga. In the fifty years of my work as a psychotherapist and teacher of growth, I have developed practices that integrate elements from all three of these traditions with insights from modern consciousness research. I call these practices *alchemical divination,* by which I mean a structured, intuitive process of accessing inner sources of healing and insight. In my work this process is sometimes, though not always, amplified by mind-assisting entheogenic substances, which have been a key interest of mine since my graduate-school days at Harvard University in the early 1960s. I have described the alchemical divination processes in my book *Ecology of Consciousness: The Alchemy of Personal, Collective, and Planetary Transformation* (2017). The present book is, in one sense, an autobiographical companion to that volume, relating key personal encounters in my lifelong quest for the healing and wisdom of the philosophers' stone.

Both Sigmund Freud and C. G. Jung, the two giants of twentieth-century psychology, used metaphors from alchemy to describe deep psychological processes that cut across the boundaries of body and mind, conscious and unconscious processes. Jung's work in particular, translating the obscure metaphors of alchemy into the language of twentieth-century psychology, has been very influential for me—although Jung did not have any direct experience with awareness-amplifying substances, focusing his attention primarily on the analysis of dream symbolism. I have also been influenced by the work of the anthropologist Michael Harner, who translated and reformulated the cross-cultural metaphors associated with the shamanic drumming journey into a distinct set of practices that can be used in modern society for obtaining guidance and healing from the spirits of nature.

European alchemy was a school of secret knowledge of transformation practices known as the Hermetic tradition. The writings and illustrations of the alchemists, which were produced in Europe in the late Middle Ages and early modern era, are notorious for their mysterious and obscure symbolism. It must be remembered that these texts were produced during a time when the Catholic Church dominated all aspects of private life. The spiritual development teachings of the Hermetic alchemists, as well as the healing practices of so-called witchcraft, had to be kept secret and disguised in obscure symbols, because of the very real danger of persecution by the enforcers of the Inquisition. So the psychological and spiritual aspects of this integrated system of knowledge and healing wisdom became dissociated from the purely material aspects, which survived and developed into what we now know as modern chemistry.

By examining some of the alchemists' mysterious utterances about the philosophers' stone, we can gain some sense of the psychospiritual meanings hidden in their obscure metaphors. The following are some of the examples I have found and cited from classic alchemical texts.

First, "stone" is matter from the mineral realm, the primordial substrate or ground of life, more basic even than cellular and organic life. In an inadvertent reference to the symbolism of the philosophers' stone, the twentieth-century drug subculture developed the expression "being stoned" to describe the state induced by psychedelic drugs, including cannabis. I suggest that the symbolism of the stone refers both to a certain immobility of the body in "stoned" states of consciousness, as well as the stillness of the mind in a meditative state.

Second, paradoxically, the *lapis* is also described as being fluid, like an essence or tincture, or sometimes a combination of stone and water. One seventeenth-century alchemical text is titled *The Sophic Hydrolith* ("The Waterstone of Wisdom"). This points to the paradox of a state of consciousness that, on the one hand, is grounded in matter, solid, and still, but on the other hand is also nonattached, flexible, and flowing, like the "watercourse way" spoken of in the ancient Chinese writings on the way of Tao.

Third, the "stone" was said to be everywhere around one in external reality and yet, not obvious and overt. "Our substance is openly displayed before the eyes of all, and yet it is not known," according to a medieval text called *The New Chemical Light.* This points to the interiority of this water-stone consciousness—it's not a specific thing "out there." It is entirely a function of the attitude and perspective we take. Another sixteenth-century text, called *Glory of the World,* says, "Our stone is found in all mountains, all trees, all herbs, all animals, and with all human beings," making it clear that the "stone" is a shared subjective quality ("our stone") combined with an objective perception.

Fourth, the "stone" is within: "This thing is extracted from you, you are its ore; . . . and when you have experienced this, the love and desire for it will be increased in you," according to the seventeenth-century author Morienus. It is a state of wisdom consciousness that can only be known by direct personal experience, the ability to be objective about the "hard facts" of a given situation, as it actually is, without illusions or distortions. It is so precious and beautiful that, having experienced it, one will have the longing and desire to magnify and express it.

This is the crux of the paradoxical and elusive nature of the philosophers' stone as an experience and its relation to language. When we know truth, we know it, at least for that moment. But truth, as we also understand, is elusive and hard to capture in language, especially when dealing with multidimensional experiences. So we resort to paradox—we say it's solid, like rock, and yet fluid, like water. And we tell stories of our search for wisdom and truth using analogies and metaphors, as we shall see in the stories told in this book. Like the Stone Age shamans and their modern descendants, we tell of the out-of-body journeys we may take to find our connection to the spirits of healing and discovery. And we tell of how we learn the language of animals, who can be our guides and companions on the search, and how we learn of the mysterious teaching plants and fungi that can help light our pathways through the dark and dense realms of conditioned matter.

In this book I tell of significant encounters with teachers that led to insights far beyond what I had anticipated or expected. During my thirties, forties, fifties, and beyond, as I immersed myself in Eastern and Western esoteric spiritual traditions, as well as the worldview of shamanistic cultures, empirical observation and tangible results led me to accept the reality of personal relationships one can have with familial or totemic animal deities and with spirit beings associated with other cultures and other realms of being. That is why in this book I have also included lessons I learned from certain animal spirits in my shamanic practice, as well as teachings associated with visionary plants and from encounters with deceased human beings in lucid dreams or meditative states.

The stories, which are all true accounts of my personal experiences, are arranged in roughly chronological order of their occurrence.

In the first chapter, I relate my classic 1960s California story of fragmenting family and community relationships, followed by an unexpected and delightful connection with Paul and Marguerite Frey, who, with their twelve children, later founded and grew the Frey family vineyards and organic and biodynamic winery. At a time of stress and turmoil in my life, I learned vital lessons from them about the alchemy of rootedness in the land and the enduring importance of family.

Chapter 2 tells the story of my relationship with Wilson Van

Dusen, my supervising psychologist at the Mendocino State Hospital, who had discovered a fascinating congruence between the auditory hallucinations of chronic schizophrenics and the spirits, good and bad, described by the eighteenth-century Swedish mystic and scientist Emanuel Swedenborg. My collegial relationship with Van Dusen continued long after we had both left the state hospital as I came to appreciate his enormously wide range of interests and insights.

In chapter 3, I relate my meeting with Morrnah Simeona, the extraordinary Hawaiian Kahuna and bodywork healer, in the 1970s. Occurring shortly after the traumatizing death of my young son, our encounter not only provided me with profound healing but also introduced me to the beautiful Hawaiian spiritual cosmology. In Hawaii at that time I also had some meetings with individuals who unexpectedly opened my mind to the possibilities of extraterrestrial contact.

In chapter 4, I describe the lessons learned from an unwelcome encounter with malignant sorcery in the context of an ayahuasca experience, which took place in the 1990s. From that encounter and its aftermath, I came to appreciate that connections with spirits, like any relationships, can be harmful as well as beneficent—and that it behooves us, as explorers and healers, to always be mindful of the possibilities of deception and exploitation.

In chapter 5, I relate the memorable conversations and correspondence I had, over the course of a thirty-year period, with Albert Hofmann, the Swiss chemist and alchemist who discovered LSD and psilocybin, and who astonished the world with his discoveries. I was deeply impressed and moved by his profoundly life-affirming mystic vision. Hofmann and I talked and exchanged letters relating to our shared interests in the mind and the promise of its expanded possibilities. For me, he was the master who opened up new pathways to an expanded cosmology for our time.

In chapter 6, I describe my experiences, during the late 1960s and 1970s, with the healing and teaching plant medicine *iboga* from central Africa, where it is used in initiation rituals. In modern times this medicine has been used with dramatic successes in the healing of long-term drug addictions. In my own experiences with it, in the form of extract tinctures, I unexpectedly discovered a connection with an African teacher spirit, a master from the astral plane who taught me profound lessons about my life and my world.

In chapter 7, I describe an encounter with a totally different kind of African spirituality. In the 1980s, some ten years after my iboga initiation experience, I had the opportunity to meet with Akuete Durchbach from Togo in West Africa, a healer-teacher whose spirit invocations and practices involve the subtle trance dances and rhythms of the original *Vodoun* religion. No substances are ingested in their ceremonies, but a workshop and subsequent conversation with Akuete provided meaningful insights into this little-known but profound spiritual tradition and practice.

In chapter 8, I tell the story of my personal involvement with the people responsible for the introduction of the extraordinary empathogenic drug MDMA, or Ecstasy, into our culture. MDMA is a perfect example of a substance that embodies the healing virtue of the philosophers' stone. It does not provide you with elaborate multidimensional visions, but it does open you to perceiving the rock-bottom reality of what is here and now—without distortion and without fear. I describe my encounters with Alexander Shulgin, the chemist inventor, and with Jack Downing and Leo Zeff, the psychotherapists who tutored me in its use in healing applications, along with some of the remarkable healing experiences that I witnessed.

Chapter 9 is devoted to an account of my MDMA therapy work in the mid-1980s with traumatized Vietnam War veteran Ed Ellis. In his reports and letters he described the healing efficacy of the resultant empathic emotional acceptance. Our correspondence continued intermittently over the next twenty years: Ed would write me from time to time, describing his growing involvement and commitment to peace work with former soldiers in the Vietnam and Iraq wars and his insights from powerful visions.

In chapter 10, I describe a visit, with a couple of friends, to the Ácoma Pueblo in New Mexico, during the Harvest Feast Day celebrations on a boiling hot day in 2002. As the drums and dancers continued all day without interruption, my friends and I unexpectedly found ourselves drawn into an extraordinary performance by a word magician, who entranced us with his telling of the traditional history of the people of this pueblo.

Chapter 11 presents an account of my friendship and conversations with the brothers Terence and Dennis McKenna over a period of more than thirty years—Terence, the storyteller and philosopher, and Dennis, the ethnobotanist and biochemist. Both of them shared my absorbing interest in shamanic and alchemical substances and practices. In our conversations and letters we reviewed their stories of youthful misadventure and madness in the Amazon jungle, followed by divergent but connected life journeys: Terence as the ironic and eloquent culture critic and Dennis as the scientist unraveling the mysteries of rainforest medicines.

Chapter 12 presents three teaching tales of encounters with animals, each of them reaching beyond natural history and ecology into the mysterious intersections of the natural and the spiritual worlds. In the first story, "Desert Tortoise Encounter," I relate how I violated ethical boundaries in relationship to a creature in its natural home— and paid a painful price for a lesson in ecological ethics. In the second story, "Whale Dreaming," I relate a number of powerful dream visions with whales that helped me overcome old feelings of insecurity and strengthened my sense of being at home in the world. In the third set of encounters, with "Lizard—Time Traveler and Trickster," I was shown how appearance and reality can be made to flit in and out from each other—as required or offered by the needs and possibilities of the moment.

In chapter 13, I relate my lifelong learning from the writings of the Greco-Armenian alchemist and mystic G. I. Gurdjieff, whom I never met since he died in 1949. When I was already in my late fifties, my connection with him through his writings unexpectedly took on a deeper level of reality after I had a series of lucid-dream meetings with him. These encounters suggested that we had known each other personally in a previous life of mine. In these lucid-dream meetings, he taught me methods and understandings that I could apply in my alchemical divination workshops. Through them I was guided much deeper in my explorations of the mysteries of life and death.

In chapter 14, I tell the story of how the accidental death of my niece's child, resonating with the memory awareness of my own son's death forty years before, triggered a soul connection with the child's spirit in the world beyond—enabling me to transmit a consoling message to her bereft parents. I provide a version of an anonymous poem, "Song of a Departed Child Spirit," that I found many years ago at the Santo Domingo Pueblo visitor center.

I have also included an appendix, "Gurdjieff and the Gnostic Gospel of Judas." I discuss a previously unknown text from the early history of Christianity, called the Gospel of Judas, that first appeared in 2006. This strange and fragmented text aroused great controversy because it portrayed the archetypal traitor in a completely different light—as one of Jesus's closest and most trusted disciples. A similarly opposite view of Judas's character and role had also been described by Gurdjieff, whose book *All and Everything: Beelzebub's Tales to His Grandson* appeared in 1950, over fifty years before the publication of this Gospel of Judas. In my essay I describe this paradoxical finding and what it might imply for our understanding of the Gnostic teacher Jesus and his disciples.

ONE

THE FREY FAMILY
WINEMAKERS

In the late 1960s I moved to San Francisco from the East Coast, where I had been living in an intentional community in Millbrook, New York. I was part of a vast movement of psychedelic pioneers and hippie pilgrims seeking a new paradise. "California Dreaming" and "All You Need Is Love" were among the anthems of this movement playing constantly on the radio. Tens of thousands of young people, and some older ones as well, moved westward with a mixture of blithe assurance and incredulity that a New Age of peace and love was at hand. "California is love," as one seventeen-year-old hitchhiking girl we met on our westward trek said with ecstatic confidence. Darker undercurrents of rage and violence were also roiling the culture—Martin Luther King Jr. and Robert Kennedy were both assassinated in 1968.

Our Millbrook community, formally organized as the Castalia Foundation, consisted of Tim Leary; his two children; Dick Alpert (later known as Ram Dass); and my wife, Susan, and me, among a dozen or so other people in a constantly changing cast of characters. Ram Dass and I, with coauthor Gary Bravo, have written about our life in this community in the conversational memoir *Birth of a Psychedelic Culture* (2010). We describe the increasingly chaotic nature of our personal lives and community interactions during the mid- to late 1960s, as the entire society and culture went through its Uranian, Neptunian, and Plutonian convulsions.

Family structures and personal relationships were seemingly dissolving as fast as new forms of community were forming. After my return from an ecstatic but overidealized spiritual pilgrimage to India, I became involved with a young woman called Barbara, who joined the Millbrook community, which itself was going through a series of severe personal and financial stresses. We tried to maintain some kind of minimal group spiritual practice, with regular meditations and programmed group psychedelic sessions. But the dispersive forces were stronger than the cohesive ones. Dick Alpert went to India on his pilgrimage, from which he returned as Ram Dass. Tim Leary got arrested in Texas and started a long ten-year odyssey of trials, more arrests, and imprisonment. He has described these various misadventures with the wit and style of a masterful Irish storyteller in his autobiography *Flashbacks* (1983).

I left the Millbrook community and moved to New York City in the fall of 1965. My departure had a lot to do with Barbara, my girlfriend, getting pregnant. A few months into the pregnancy, she underwent an abrupt and complete personality change: she lost her infatuation with me and also lost all interest in the Hindu-tinged meditation practices that our Millbrook community was trying to maintain. She wanted to shop and buy clothes and hang out and listen to music. She met a light-show artist called Richard Aldcroft who had a paying job as a Madison Avenue advertising designer and became entranced with him. On one of our trips to the city, she moved in with him and said to me, "I'm not coming back with you." She was six months pregnant with my child.

Despite the blow to my male ego from her abrupt departure, Barbara and I did maintain a tentatively cordial relationship and commitment to the Millbrook program of exploring psychedelic experience. During her home birth, she ingested a small amount, less than 100 micrograms, of LSD. She reported—like other women who did this—that though she could feel the contractions, they somehow weren't quite as painful, because there were many other interesting and varied sensations going on, and there was no resistance in her body or her attitude. Of course that meant the baby was born on LSD—supersensitive, and not in an anesthetic haze.

I moved from Millbrook to New York City in large part to try to generate some income so I could assume responsibility for the child, whom we named Ari Krishna. The Millbrook community was broke, and so was I. It was my time of what astrologers call the Saturn return, associated with the return of the planet Saturn to its natal position in the horoscope—the period of around twenty-seven to thirty-two years of age. During this time, we normally move out of the formative years of childhood, youth, and early adulthood into the middle years of marriage, practicing a profession, raising children, and participating in community. My life trajectory had none of those elements. I had no job or income and no place to live, with a child whose mother left me and a community of friends that was disbanded. I was working on artistic performance projects with very little or no pay.

Shortly after Ari was born, Barbara and her partner split up, and she left Ari with her parents, who lived in the Bronx and referred to their daughter as an "alley cat." She left for England with a New York rock group. Six months later, the group threw her out. When she returned, her parents refused to give the child back to her, considering her an unfit mother. She enlisted my help. There were hysterical confrontations, with the infant literally being pulled between competing pairs of arms. Eventually we did persuade her parents to release Ari back to her and my shared custody. We worked out shared childcare arrangements, but with much drama and anxiety. Barbara had the habit of abruptly changing her mind: "You take him now, it's too much for me"—or "No, I want him now." Nonetheless, my paternal bond with Ari thrived, even as my co-parenting with his mother deteriorated in uncertainty, anxiety, and frustration.

When I first moved to California in 1967, I lived in Tim Leary's old house in the Berkeley hills while trying to find my financial footing. There was a changing cast of characters here as well: refugees from the dispersed Millbrook community and the East Coast scene. Through my friendship and connection with Robert Mogar, who was a psychology professor at San Francisco State University and a supporter of our Millbrook-based writing and publishing projects, I obtained a contract to give a series of lectures to the staff at Mendocino State Hospital (MSH) in Ukiah on the psychopharmacology of psychedelic drugs. The popular casual tripping use of these drugs was on the rise, and psychiatric clinics and hospitals were beginning to see "bad trip" casualties requiring pharmacological intervention and at times temporary hospitalization. I had the educational credentials of my postdoctoral fellowship in pharmacology at the Harvard Medical School, and had written a lengthy review article on the pharmacology of psychedelic drugs for the first issue of the *Psychedelic Review*. I was happy to have the small income from the lectures and drove the three-hour trip from Berkeley to Talmage, near Ukiah, once a week for the next six weeks.

Mendocino State Hospital was a sprawling campus of buildings, built in 1889 as a hospital for the "criminally insane." By the late 1950s it had a resident patient population of three thousand chronic psychotics and alcoholics. As I discovered, it had several progressive treatment programs and innovative staff training programs. This was in the era before the newer medications. The treatment drug of choice for psychosis was Thorazine, which had the disconcerting side-effect of turning patients' skin a blotchy purple color.

I started to travel up to MSH for a couple of days each week. I would stay in one of the guest cottages on the hospital grounds, and I remember sometimes being woken at night by the blood-curdling screams of poor souls tormented by the demons of their dreams. When, after some time, I was offered a full-time position as a clinical psychologist at the hospital, I was glad to be able to move off campus to a more tranquil location.

Sometime during the few months that I had stayed in Leary's house in Berkeley, commuting up to Ukiah a couple of times a week, starting to put my life back into order, and earning a small salary, Barbara arrived with Ari, who was by then about four or five months old. She left him with me, claiming that she could not take care of him. I felt a huge relief and joy at being able to bond with my son more completely, along with considerable anxiety about how I was going to take care of him while moving more and more time up to Ukiah to work at the MSH.

Having been traumatized in my male-provider ego, I had not developed an ongoing relationship with a woman who could help me take care of the infant. A therapist I was working with wisely (and obviously) suggested that I needed to separate the roles of girlfriend and child caretaker.

This was the project I was working on when I moved up north to Ukiah to start at the Mendocino State Hospital in my first serious paying job. Wilson Van Dusen, the head of the psychology department and my supervisor, introduced me to Paul Frey, a psychiatrist at the hospital, who lived with his wife Marguerite ("Beba") Frey, also an M.D., and their eleven children, on a ranch and vineyard in Redwood Valley.

I was looking both for a place to live and for someone to help me take care of my infant son. It turned out that the Frey family ranch had a one-bedroom cottage very near their main house that I could rent. When I told Paul Frey and Van Dusen about my need for childcare while I was working at the hospital, Beba generously offered to let Ari stay with them during the day. Even when she herself was not there, there were always older teenage children in the family who could look after him as well as their own younger siblings. My relief and gratitude was profound. I could hardly believe my blessed good fortune.

Ari was crying quite a bit during this phase. He had been moved around a lot. Beba immediately tuned in and saw that because he was still in the crawling stage, he felt a bit left out of the action of the older kids, who were running and playing all around him. She then assigned Mimi, at fourteen the oldest of the girls, and one of her sisters to take turns holding Ari and carrying him around. After only a couple more weeks, he asked to be let down and was participating energetically in the games and activities of the other kids. There may have been some, but certainly not much, jealousy at the new interloper among the Frey children. But the striking thing to us adults was that Ari looked just like everyone else—blond and blue-eyed. He thrived in that protective environment of goodwill, affection, and creative exuberance. For me, a long bad dream of separation and insecurity seemed to be coming to an end. But not quite yet, as it turned out.

Paul Frey, then in his fifties, was a maverick among the staff doctors at Mendocino State Hospital. His younger colleagues were amused at his personal mannerisms, like walking around the hospital in his country boots, as well as at his forceful and blunt speech. But they respected the way he handled his assignment, one that nobody else wanted: the wards with the most chronic and regressed psychotics, considered untreatable

Fig. 1.1. Wilson Van Dusen (left) and Paul Frey at Frey Ranch, 1978.
Photo by Ralph Metzner

and hospitalized for life. He told me that after years of practice, he had concluded that the best he could do for these people was to provide a safe environment and encourage them to relax and enjoy their madness. He did not support the practice of turning them into walking vegetables with massive doses of Thorazine, and he was supportive of younger interns or psychologists like me who wanted to try psychological approaches that were inspired in part by our explorations with psychedelics.

Paul himself would tend to their medical needs, and he was always receptive to any of the patients who really wanted to talk with him. But it was not uncommon for him to dismiss someone by saying, "If you're going to talk real crazy like that, go away. Come back when you want to talk straight." On the female ward they had a beat-up old piano, and sometimes he'd sit down and play old-fashioned honky-tonk tunes, to the great delight of the older women, who would crowd around him in their housecoats, some with their skin blotched purple from Thorazine, clapping their hands and laughing. His only rule was that they were not to touch him. He told me this was to protect him from the "smearers," who would sidle up in a friendly way with a "hello, deary," and wipe a fistful of fecal matter on your arm or shoulder.

Paul relished the lunatic logic and outrageous humor of some of his charges. He roared with laughter as he told the story of the woman patient he'd observed from the window bending down in the yard, picking up invisible worms and holding them up triumphantly. When he asked her why she was picking up the worms, she replied with regal dignity, "I'm the queen of the birds."

Paul came from a long line of Lutheran ministers living in the New York area. His grandfather had immigrated from Germany in the 1880s. He was well read in German literature, history, and philosophy and liked to speak to me in German, greeting me with *guter alter Freund*. He had studied for the Lutheran ministry, like his father, but when he told his examiners at the end of his studies that he intended to go on to medicine, not to the ministry, they refused to ordain him, claiming he lacked sufficient commitment for the church.

Marguerite "Beba" Frey was born and raised Brooklyn in 1924, also the daughter of a Lutheran minister. From her early life on, she preferred rural living and working on a farm. She also became a medical doctor, and after she and Paul married and started their family, they found positions in various places, gradually moving west across the country. They spent a few years practicing medicine on the Navajo reservation in Arizona, and absorbed much of the natural and grounded spirituality of these indigenous Americans. When I met them at Mendocino State Hospital, Paul was on the ward for adult chronic psychotics and geriatrics, and Beba worked on the pediatrics ward. Her professional life and family life seemed to mesh effortlessly. After the MSH closed, she took a position at the Sonoma State Hospital in Glen Ellen.

Bob Mogar, along with me and several of the other psychologists and medical students interning at Mendocino State Hospital, would often spend time at the Frey ranch, talking with Paul, Beba, and their children (eleven of them at the time, but who would eventually number twelve). There were long afternoons and weekend times with stimulating conversations, with Paul holding forth in grand style, telling stories and philosophizing.

When at home, Beba would be cooking, cleaning, and taking care of the household, always good-natured, with clusters of children in twos, threes, or fours running around and playing. I have a memory image of her standing by the stove, stirring a pot of soup, holding the youngest child in the pre-toddler stage on her hip, sometimes wiping the floor with one foot on a cloth. After we had become friends, I once asked her why she chose to have so many children. She replied that childbearing was easy for her, and she was scientifically fascinated by seeing the different expressions of the same two sets of parental genes. Paul's attitude was a little different. He said he was not that interested in the smaller children until they were old enough to talk with, and he just went along with what Beba wanted.

When I first started to hang out there, I was amazed that Beba never seemed to worry or fuss about the children running around, gleefully screaming, as children do, barefoot in a yard filled with old pieces of wood or metal and other potentially sharp objects. I realized that if something happened, she would take care of it—she was a medical doctor after all—and worrying about it would not contribute to anyone's safety.

They lived in a huge converted barn, with old-fashioned wooden bar locks, on a hundred-acre ranch that Paul had planted with grapes, preparing for the time when he could retire from psychiatry and devote himself to his winery. He anticipated working with his children on the family ranch and vineyard when they were grown. The place was strewn with pieces of old machinery, saw blades, metal pipes and scraps, pieces of lumber, and artifacts that Paul used to pick up from junkyards for possible future uses. He liked to call himself an "archaeologist of the present."

When Paul was walking around his ranch, inspecting his grapes, or discoursing at length to his students about the forest ecosystem, he was in his element. With his wide-brimmed black hat, his red beard, and his ever-present pipe, he reminded me of Van Gogh, his mind fired up with wild images. Or in the evenings, by the fireplace in his rough-hewn room, filled to the brim with junkyard artifacts and books, he would hold forth about his favorite author—Pierre Teilhard de Chardin. He was deeply interested in applying some of Teilhard's ideas to the problems of mind-body interaction. He thought the superconductive phenomena exhibited by some substances at very low temperatures provided a good analogy to the thought processes of the mind. He was always discoursing about "superconductivity at room temperature." He wrote a poem, called "Lines Written on Reading Father Teilhard de Chardin," which I published in the *Psychedelic Review,* number 10. Here are some lines from it:

> *And the light became flesh*
> *See them! The shining, eternal interfaces*
> *Sparkling and crackling,*
> *Pleistocene lightning bolts*
> *In the gray, cold glacier clouds.*

And down below a silent, fur-clad early
*   mind-substrate*
Tongues of fire in his head
Of the far future,
Stares into the flames and the flashes,
The hot red curlings and spirals leap through his eyes
Into his head—just one spark.
And the fire-echoes sweep through icy charged brain
*   furnaces*
Ignition incarnate. Incarnation!

Paul himself had never taken LSD, but in the late 1950s he had participated as medical supervisor in studies done by Wilson Van Dusen and in the experiments of Fritz Perls, which inspired some of the latter's formulations regarding Gestalt therapy. To me, Paul epitomized the forest-philosopher or scholar-farmer of an old European type, living in a Black Forest village. Self-sufficient yet interdependent with family and neighbors, grounded in God's earth, yet with a visionary view of the times and possibilities to come. Being around the Freys and their high-spirited and hard-working family life was a welcome respite for me from the chaos and confusion of the 1960s psychedelic culture.

I had been living as a neighbor of the Frey family for six to eight months when one day Barbara (or Jennifer as she was now calling herself) showed up with a slender, long-haired man in his midtwenties, coming to see Ari, as they declared. I was surprised and somewhat anxious, having heard nothing from her in many months, but I invited them in, offered them tea, and invited them to stay for dinner and overnight. I then drove off by myself to the village market to buy more food. When I came back, my house was empty—they and Ari were gone. I panicked and rushed over to the Freys' home, where Jonathan, the oldest, who was then about sixteen, had insisted that they stay and wait till I, as well as Beba and Paul, came home. Later I told him I would never forget his simple act of generosity and common sense, which saved a bad situation from turning even worse.

It was a weekend, and there were several visitors from San Francisco on the ranch, all of whom witnessed this drama of attempted but prevented kidnapping. To Jennifer and her partner, I raged and raved: you show no interest in your child for eight months, not a word, and then show up, and abuse my hospitality and trust by trying to kidnap him! She could have asked to work out a sharing arrangement, after all. She had chosen to stay completely out of touch.

As it happened, my stay in the psychology department at Mendocino State Hospital had come to an end. I had a job offer at the psychology department of a newly opened Kaiser medical facility in Hayward. I was glad I had not told Jennifer and took off, asking my friends at the Frey ranch not to reveal my whereabouts to the pair. I drove off in my van to the south, with Ari, always of good cheer and ready for adventure. I found a place to live in the south Peninsula, across the bridge from Hayward, and started to work at Kaiser, finding a day-care facility for Ari.

This was not the last of a series of bizarre twists and turns between Jennifer and me around Ari, including kidnapping, that drove me to the edge of madness and despair. I will not tell that story here. Eventually my open conflict with her subsided, and we worked out a commonsense shared childcare system. Ultimately, however, it was a tragic story, because Ari died in an accident with his bicycle when he was eight years old.

In retrospect, the time around his first two years, staying at the fantastic and magical Frey ranch and playing, learning, and growing with his twelve seeming siblings, may have been a high point in his soul's journey on Earth this time. Twenty years later, in the 1990s, I had a dream unexpectedly connecting Ari's story with the Frey family, whom we both knew when he was a very young child.

I'm with my mother and father, meeting with Mimi Frey and her fiancé, Steve, at a café. I'm telling my parents about who she is, about her family, and about how she and her sisters and mother used to take care of Ari when we were neighbors and he was two or three. In the dream Mimi is in her twenties, though in reality she was in her forties at that time.

As I reflected on this dream it occurred to me that perhaps Ari had reincarnated in the Frey family. From my reading of the literature on reincarnation memories, I knew that it was not uncommon when a child died, the soul might choose a next life that was somehow connected, through family or place, to the previous life that was cut short. The presence of my parents, Ari's grandparents, in the dream meeting was consistent with that. Grandparents always seem to care and want to know and stay in touch with grandchildren—whether in this life or the next. It occurred to me that Ari had benefited so much from his brief stay with the Frey family as an infant that he wanted to develop those soul connections further in another life.

Fig. 1.2. Beba Frey in 1994, at the winery compound.
Photo by Ralph Metzner

I visited the Frey ranch in the Redwood Valley in 1994 to tell my friends about this dream vision. I talked with Beba and Mimi, the oldest daughter, as well as several of the other now-adult children, who remembered Ari as a childhood playmate. They immediately resonated with the possibility of a reincarnation connection and started to go through a mental list of which of the many grandchildren it could probably be. We weren't trying to prove anything, but we finally settled on Tyler, one of Adam Frey's three children. Tyler is a Leo, and in one of my dreams with the Frey family, I had seen two lions romping around the field. I took a photo of the ten-year-old Tyler, playing on the ground in a mud patch. It is said the eyes are the windows of the soul, carrying soul memories of other lives. In Tyler's eyes I could see Ari also looking through. Because of what I shared, both his parents and Tyler himself have serenely accepted Ari's soul presence in their life.

I stayed in touch with the Frey family, visiting every few years, delighting in the changes as the children grew into adults and started families of their own. Paul Frey passed away in 1990, when he was in his late sixties or early seventies. By that time, his older children had grown and learned enough and had gradually taken over the family vineyards. Jonathan and Matthew Frey, along with Jonathan's wife, Katrina, used the original vines planted by Paul to start a family winery, producing a series of prize-winning wines under the Frey label. Many of the original siblings and their spouses and children still work full-time at the Frey winery.

In 1980 Frey Vineyards became the first organic and biodynamic winery in the United States. Biodynamics is based on the work of the early twentieth-century Austrian philosopher and educator Rudolf Steiner. Basically it involves attending to and furthering subtle ecological and cosmic forces by adding minute doses of various plant and animal products to the soil and timing the planting and harvest cycles in accord with seasonal and lunar cycles.

Besides their designated main role in the family business, each of the siblings, as well as their spouses and grown children, play various different roles during harvest and planting times, as needed. Stimulated no doubt by our personal connection, my family and I are happy consumers of Frey organic, sulfite-free and biodynamic wines. Their website is freywine.com.

———

As I reflect on the significance of my connection in the 1960s with the Frey family and their vineyards, in addition to the personal assistance the Frey family offered me, they embodied and exemplified an older and more traditional kind of culture during a time of chaotic social transformation. In the sixties many of the old cultural models were falling apart under the impact of despised foreign wars, civil-rights protests, feminist and environmental movements, the sexual revolution, and, not least, the spread of mind-expanding substances. During these years the Frey family nevertheless managed to establish a home-grown, cooperative, and progressive family business. I will always cherish the memories of my connection with them.

TWO

WILSON VAN DUSEN— MYSTIC NAVIGATOR

The chief psychologist and my supervisor at Mendocino State Hospital during my time there was Wilson Van Dusen (1923–2005), who turned out to be one of the most interesting people I have ever met. Over the years we were in regular contact, I kept discovering further unexpected aspects of his many-faceted interests and skills. He was one of the first psychologists to explore the connections between Eastern meditation practices and psychotherapy, publishing a paper in a professional journal in 1958 titled "Wu Wei, No-Mind, and the Fertile Void in Psychotherapy." He experimented with low-dose LSD sessions in the early 1960s (before it was made illegal) independently of and before our studies at Harvard and their subsequent notoriety. He published a paper in a psychiatric journal on the parallels between LSD experience and Zen Buddhist meditative states, entitled "LSD and the Enlightenment of Zen."

Van Dusen had trained in and practiced Gestalt therapy, and he had worked collaboratively with Fritz Perls in developing that approach. He told me privately that the early experiments with low-dose LSD that he and Perls did together directly led to some of the first formulations of the Gestalt approach. *Gestalt* is a German word meaning "form" or "shape." The chief feature distinguishing that approach to therapy from psychoanalysis is consideration of the form of the interaction, not just the meaning content of the words involved. Van Dusen used his hands to make shapes in talking about these formal patterns of interaction and relationship.

Van Dusen, or "Van" as he was called by his colleagues, was also a recognized authority on Emmanuel Swedenborg (1688–1772), the great Swedish scientist, inventor, cosmologist, philosopher, theologian, and clairvoyant mystic, who wrote voluminously on scientific and spiritual topics. After spending the first forty years of his life as a physical scientist and engineer, Swedenborg started to receive what he called "visitations," in which he conversed with angels and spirits, applying his disciplined powers of observation to developing a detailed cartography of the nonmaterial realms. Van Dusen had studied Swedenborg's writings intensively and asked himself whether Swedenborgian concepts could help him understand the inner life of his psychotic patients. He had published an essay in a psychology journal in the early 1960s entitled "The Presence of Spirits in Madness." This was later expanded into a book called *The Presence of Other Worlds*.

Swedenborg distinguished between higher-order spirits (traditionally called angels), whose messages were inspiring and benevolent, and lower-order spirits (traditionally called demons), whose messages and voices were malevolent and demeaning. Chronic schizophrenics are generally considered to be inaccessible by any coherent form of conversation, but Van Dusen took a phenomenological approach in talking with them. Instead of dismissing their hallucinations and voices as meaningless cerebral waste matter, Van Dusen talked to the hospitalized patients with respect and asked them to translate for him what the voices were saying. He wrote, "I treat the hallucinations as realities, because that is what they are to the patient." One of his most consistent findings was that the patients objected to the term *hallucination*—they felt they had real contact with another world or order of beings.

As he listened with empathy to his patients' descriptions of their voices, Van Dusen, like Swedenborg, noted that it was possible to distinguish helpful, positive voices from critical, judgmental ones, the latter being the majority. He coached his patients to listen to the rarer positive voices and as much as possible to ignore the judgmental ones. With this approach he obtained some noticeably positive results in a population notorious for being untreatable.

Swedenborg had described in detail his own controlled visits to heaven and hell. He wrote in his journal that he "felt gifted by the Lord with the experience of heaven and hell and could examine over a period of many years their exact relationship to man." Van Dusen wrote that "psychosis always involves some degree of self pride (spiritual madness), but the hallucinated aspect looks most like what Swedenborg described under the general heading of obsessions and possessions." Van Dusen's findings from his interviews with schizophrenics corresponded closely with what Swedenborg had said about the lower-order "evil spirits" and how they can take over a person, causing him to lose his memory of other aspects of his personality. On the other hand, "the higher-order hallucinations are quite a bit rarer, and do not oppose the patient's will, but rather are helpful guides, and are more abstract, symbolic, and creative than the lower order hallucinations. In Swedenborg's terms the higher order would be angels who come to assist the person. As Swedenborg describes it, they reside in the interior mind which does not think in words but in universals."

I was delighted to meet with Van Dusen and discover his enormous range of interests. We were in alignment in our views toward so-called mental illness, regarding it not so much as a disease, but rather as a loss of one's spiritual center, while having somehow become opened to nonordinary realms of consciousness along with much fear and confusion. His approach accorded totally with the empathic approach I had developed toward psychotic states of consciousness, whether they were endogenous or had been induced by drugs.

As I discovered from our conversations, during World War II Van Dusen had served in the U.S. Coast Guard and spent three years in the merchant marine. During his time at sea, he became expert in celestial navigation and was licensed as second mate and radar observer in the United States, and as captain for all oceans. He worked as a training officer for the U.S. Coast Guard Academy for fifteen years. For years after I had left Mendocino State Hospital, we kept in touch, and I kept learning of more of his varied fields of interest and expertise. When I visited him once at his home in Ukiah, I learned that he was also an expert target shooter, with a collection of antique pistols.

We exchanged correspondence from time to time. In the early 1980s Van wrote to me with a totally unexpected invitation. It turned out that he was a member of a modern chivalric order that was directly descended from the original order of the Knights Templar, the medieval warrior-monks who took vows of poverty and obedience and protected pilgrims on the way to the Holy Land during the Crusades of the eleventh and twelfth centuries. Reading about their history, I learned that the Templars had accumulated great wealth and developed the foundations of an international banking system. After they were persecuted and disbanded by the French king in the fourteenth century, the Templars became an underground civilian, commercial, and ceremonial order. Many of their affiliated orders and families had acquired considerable wealth and property in several European countries—and rumors of secret wealth and power continue to swirl around their former role and heritage.

I did not know that this order still existed and that its activities had become entirely nonmilitary. Van Dusen invited me to apply for membership in what was now essentially a ceremonial esoteric order of socially beneficial and humane service, with an interest in history and genealogy. Van Dusen coached me through the process of formally applying for and joining this ancient order in its contemporary form. The process involved studying the history of the Templars and writing responses to a series of questions about the inner meaning of the Templar symbolism and how my present interests and activities might relate to contemporary social and environmental values. For my final thesis qualifying me for admission to the order, I wrote an essay, "The Esoteric Symbolism of the Temple," which was published in the journal of The Augustan Society, located in Southern California.

Although I have not remained active in the order, I came to appreciate the deeper understanding of certain undercurrents of European history that Van Dusen's invitation opened up for me. In my essay I wrote, "In esoteric teachings, the human body and personality are regarded symbolically as the temple of the indwelling Divine Spirit. Body and personality are inherited as raw material from the parents, and imprinted with the cultural conditioning obtaining at the time and the place of our arising—these are the so-called 'rough stones' of the temple builders." The word *temple* derives from Latin *templum,* a clear, open space marked off by the augurs for the purpose of divination. The word relates etymologically to *contemplation,* a balanced, harmonious, prayerlike mental activity; and also, suggestively, to the *temples* at the left and right sides of the forehead, anatomical seats of the brain activity of contemplation.

In my essay, I related a vivid dream I had had as a twelve-year-old boy. At the time, in 1948, I was a war refugee from Germany, living in a boarding school in the north of Scotland, several days' worth of travel away from my dispersed family, learning to understand and speak a new language. I was shy, depressed, and lonely. One day I woke up unexpectedly feeling blessed and encouraged by the following dream:

I find myself in an open temple space with columns, in which the marble floor is covered with intricate geometric patterns. To one side are six tall, humanlike figures, wearing capes of an extraordinarily luminous blue color, sitting perfectly still, and contemplating the geometric patterns on the floor. I am overcome with awe and a feeling of profound peace.

It seemed clear to me in retrospect that my inner guides had granted me this vision of a temple of wisdom to encourage me in my loneliness.

Van Dusen and I had a strange falling-out in the late 1990s, when, after some friendly correspondence, I sent him a copy of my newly published book *The Unfolding Self—Varieties of Transformative Experience.* I had chosen the title to echo William James's classic work of comparative mysticism of a hundred years earlier—*The Varieties of Religious Experience.* In a letter Van expressed an almost visceral aversion to my comparative approach to religious experience. The negativity of his reaction surprised me, and I think it surprised him as well. He was particularly drawn to the experience of unity and had himself written a book on the mystical path of oneness. The multiplicity of experiential metaphors described in my book seemed to confuse or even offend him. After this break, neither of us renewed our conversations or correspondence. But I did not let our minor doctrinal difference diminish my regard for him as a person and a philosopher; nor, I believe, did he.

In an autobiographical statement he wrote in the last year of his life (referring to himself in the third person), Van Dusen said that "he was really seven people . . . was a poet with a lifetime of experience in the arts (and) . . . a mystic with experiences of the Divine from infancy." When he was at the university, stimulated by the work of Albert Einstein, he had written a thesis on five-, six-, and seven-dimensional space. "No one

Fig. 2.1. Wilson Van Dusen with friends Charles Grob and Gary Bravo in 1998. Notice Knighthood plaques and emblems on wall. Photo by Ralph Metzner

Fig. 2.2. Van Dusen and Ralph Metzner in Ukiah, 1998

would publish it, so he put it aside for fifty years. . . . Before he passed over, he sat at his desk wrestling with the ultimates of existence. He fully expects to die before the world notices they already exist in seven-dimensional space."

Van Dusen had signed up with a hospice, and when he received its package of materials including pages on the "Signs and Symptoms of Approaching Death," he noted this with approval, but added that although it described a "sensible progression in dying," it was not conceived in any order. "So I re-wrote it and sent it to them. I fear they will cut out all the next world part. But I'll submit it anyway." He made these comments in his last letter, which began: "Dear Friends and Family—Though I am within a few days of leaving this world behind, I am having a wonderful time."

THREE

MORRNAH SIMEONA— HAWAIIAN KAHUNA AND HEALER

In November 1974 I traveled to Honolulu to give some talks and an introductory workshop on a meditation practice called Actualism. I had been invited to lecture at Windward Community College and at a local bookstore. The November 18 edition of the *Honolulu Star-Bulletin* had an article about me headlined "The Man Who Channels Light and Energy," written by Jocelyn Fujii.

> True to the tradition of teachers in esoteric disciplines, Ralph Metzner, who arrived Wednesday to lead a workshop on meditation, had almost nothing to say about it. But although he wouldn't discuss his meditation techniques on the premise that they should initially be experienced with a trainer, he had much to say about results. . . .
>
> The training, Metzner explained, is designed to produce an experience "in which a person learns how to go within and tap certain sources of energies—light-fire energies—and use those energies in problem-solving and everyday life." . . .
>
> The teaching is a modern version of a discipline that in ancient India was called *agni yoga,* or the yoga of fire, he explained. Developed by Russell Paul Schofield more than 30 years ago, Actualism is said

The Man Who Channels Light and Energy

By Jocelyn Fujii, Star-Bulletin Writer

Ask a Zen master about Zen and he'll tell you nothing.

Ask a meditator about meditation and he, too, may tell you nothing.

True to the tradition of teachers in esoteric disciplines, Ralph Metzner, who arrived Wednesday to lead a workshop on meditation, had almost nothing to say about it.

But although he wouldn't discuss his meditation techniques on the premise that they should initially be experienced with a trainer, he had much to say about results.

"We had elementary school students (5 years and older) who started off their day by sitting quietly and doing light work for 15 or 20 minutes, then they'd go about their work," he said of a one-year pilot program he conducted on the Mainland.

"THEY LOVE IT. It makes them feel good, and it's something they can do when they feel bad."

Metzner has seen astounding changes—marked academic improvement, emotional adjustment, relinquishing of drugs—through the practice of Actualism, a teaching that deals with channeling light and energy, and the subject his workshops are really about.

He conducted an experimental workshop last night at Leeward Community College as part of Windward Community College's symposium on Learning Through Altered States of Consciousness and, tomorrow, he will give an introductory lecture and demonstration on Actualism at noon at Central Bookstore, 1419 Kapiolani Blvd.

He also will offer workshops tomorrow, Sunday and Monday evenings. Those interested should call Brooke Nelson, 955-3856, for information.

THE TRAINING, Metzner explained, is designed to produce an experience "in which the person learns how to go within and tap certain sources of energy—light-fire energies—and use those energies in problem-solving and everyday life."

Although he wouldn't discuss techniques—"It has to be taught person-to-person"—he said the tools are simple, practical and workable for even those who have done no previous spiritual work.

The teaching is a modern version of a discipline that in ancient India was called agni yoga, or the yoga of fire, he explained. Developed by Russell Paul Schofield more than 30 years ago, Actualism is said to be an effective way of clearing mental or emotional pain, which is nothing more than obstructions or imbalances in the body's energy flow, allowing more inner and interpersonal harmony in daily life.

METZNER HAS BEEN a student of Actualism for six years and a teacher for three. He wrote "The Psychedelic Experience" with Timothy Leary and Richard Alpert soon after their days at Harvard when the three were experimenting with and exploring possibilities of psychedelic drugs in enhancing creativity and understanding.

Metzner was then working on his Ph.D. on child development psychology and later explored meditation, yoga and other approaches to altering consciousness.

Eventually, he said, he came upon Actualism, and the changes in his life were immeasurable.

"I used to work with drugs a lot. For five or six years I worked with psychedelics. I haven't used them at all since I began working with Actualism. I found that by working with light energy, you can alter consciousness in a way much more effective than drugs."

IN HIS BOOK "Maps of Consciousness," Metzner gives some agni yoga exercises that are used in Actualism training. In one exercise, the person is asked to sit upright in a chair, with legs apart and uncrossed,

feet flat on the ground and hands on legs. The body should be comfortable and relaxed.

The person then thinks of a point of white light located six inches above the center of the head. He thinks of the point of light as "opening up and pouring down over the body."

The exercise, performed daily and with an understanding of the laws of energy behind it, can effect profound results in internal and external balance and well-being.

IF THERE IS physical discomfort, Metzner continues in the book, the person can clear it by focusing and directing the white light energy to the point of discomfort.

The exercises and concept are dynamic, he said, with emphasis on discovering, moving and externalizing the energy flow rather than just stilling and emptying the mind. This aspect, plus the fact that the discipline includes work on the body rather than withdrawal from it, he said, distinguishes Actualism from traditional concepts of meditation.

Ralph Metzner—Photo by Ken Sakamoto

Fig. 3.1. *Honolulu Star-Bulletin* article

to be an effective way of clearing mental or emotional pain, caused by obstructions and imbalances in the body's energy flow, allowing more inner and interpersonal harmony in daily life.

Metzner has been a student of Actualism for six years and a teacher for three. He wrote *The Psychedelic Experience* with Timothy Leary and Richard Alpert soon after their days at Harvard when the three were experimenting with and exploring possibilities of psychedelic drugs in enhancing creativity and understanding.

Metzner was then working on his Ph.D. on child development psychology and later explored meditation, yoga and other approaches to altering consciousness. "I used to work with drugs a lot. For five or six years I worked with psychedelics. I haven't used them at all since I began working with Actualism. I found that by working with light energy, you can alter consciousness in a way much more effective than drugs."

So this was my self-presentation, my public persona, at that time, in my midthirties: I had experimented with mind-expanding drugs in the 1960s and was now using meditation techniques to accomplish the similar purpose of expanding and heightening consciousness. Forty years later, as I was writing this story, it was a little strange for me to reread the journalistic account of my presentation. I still agree with the basic stance expressed in the interview—that meditation practices are safer and perhaps in the long run more effective ways to expand consciousness than certain drugs. But, like quite a few other meditation teachers in various traditions, I have come to a more nuanced position about consciousness-expanding substances.

Psychedelic drugs and plant substances *can* provide a preview of possibilities of expanded consciousness that are otherwise hard to obtain except after years of meditation practice. I was one of numerous explorers who made pilgrimages to Hindu or Buddhist or Sufi or Western meditation teachers that were initially stimulated by the seekers' experiences with psychedelics. Some spent several years in monasteries and meditation teacher-training programs. A recent anthology of contemporary Western Buddhist writings on psychedelics, *Zig Zag Zen* (2015), exemplifies these more differentiated perspectives. But in the midseventies, psychedelic drugs had been stigmatized as dangerous, and they were illegal; possession carried heavy penalties. Even to discuss them with positive interest was to invite academic and journalistic opprobrium.

There is one additional fact about the year 1974—a synchronicity that I only registered with surprise as I began to write about my meeting with the Kahuna Morrnah Simeona. In October 1974, one month before my visit to Hawaii, my eight-year-old son Ari had died in a bicycle accident—the most traumatic and devastating event of my life. There was of course no reason this occurrence would have come up in my public presentations and interviews at that time, and I am certain that I did not talk to the journalist from the Honolulu newspaper about the recent death of my son. I was in what I would now recognize as a post-traumatic stress reaction, which meant that I had developed a kind of protective dissociation from the traumatizing trigger event, enabling me to function normally without collapsing into grief and despair.

Such a sealing off of the traumatic event-memory enables a traumatized individual to function in ordinary life while appearing outwardly normal. At the time, however, I had no understanding of the nature of this dissociative trauma reaction and no awareness that I was in that altered state of consciousness. In fact the whole concept of post-traumatic stress disorder (PTSD) didn't really develop in the field of psychology until the late 1970s and 1980s. It is still not well understood. Dissociation is a very peculiar process. It is not at all like the Freudian concept of repression, by which the conscious ego supposedly keeps primitive childish or animalistic impulses in check. I had full recall of everything that had happened, but the painful emotions triggered by the event had been sealed off. The disconnect was so effective that I could function outwardly without being overwhelmed by this devastating blow to my psychic equilibrium.

In retrospect I cannot help wondering whether my interactions with Morrnah Simeona (1913–1992), which took place after my public talk and workshop, were somehow related to that tragedy. I do not know whether someone from the Actualism community had told her about my son's death—I know I didn't. Perhaps the unusual degree of empathic generosity that she seemed to display toward me was somehow related to that tragedy, which had occurred only a month before. The professional literature dealing with therapy for PTSD (for example, in

Fig. 3.2. Morrnah Simeona. Photo courtesy of The Foundation of I, Inc. Freedom of the Cosmos and Self I-Dentity through Ho'oponopono®

the writings of Peter Levine, Ph.D.) avers that one of the basic principles of healing trauma is not to directly activate the pain-filled memories of the trauma, but to focus the person's attention on ordinary events, as well as on ordinary bodily sensations and movements of the breath, in order to "titrate" the person's capacity to endure these devastatingly intense feelings and memories.

I had made an appointment to meet with Morrnah Simeona sometime after I was finished with my public talks. Knowing of her reputation as a bodywork healer, I had asked for a session with her—ostensibly to help me with some chronic muscular contractions in my hip and abdomen that dated to an appendix operation in my childhood. She picked me up at the hotel where I was staying, and we drove to the place where she did her bodywork sessions. She was driving a white Mercedes sports convertible, with the top down, which she said was given to her for her use by the owner, a grateful client of hers, when he was out of town. So here came an unexpected peak experience for me—I was being driven through Honolulu in a white convertible on a sparkling sunny day by a smiling, laughing, gray-haired Hawaiian woman in her late fifties.

She was telling me stories all the time—before, during, and after my bodywork session. I do not remember talking much at all. I certainly did not tell her about my son or his death—I couldn't. She told me that while she was working as a massage therapist at the Royal Hawaiian hotel, she treated many prominent people from the United States, the Far East, and Europe—heads of state, royalty, and business executives. According to Wikipedia,

> Morrnah Simeona was a practitioner of *lomilomi* massage and for 10 years owned and operated health spas at the Kahala Hilton and Royal Hawaiian hotels. Among her massage clients at the Hilton spa were Lyndon Johnson, Jackie Kennedy, and Arnold Palmer. Her mother, Lilia, was one of the last recognized *kahuna la'au kahea* or priest who heals with words. In 1983, Morrnah was recognized

as a *kahuna lapa'au* (healer) and honored as a "Living Treasure of Hawaii" by the Honpa Hongwanji Mission of Hawaii.

The *lomilomi* massage method, which I had not experienced before, includes, along with traditional strokes, a kind of gentle rocking motion of the limbs, which seem to shake out the pain-contracted tension patterns embedded in the long muscles of the limbs. I became immersed in a deeply peaceful healing trance. I do not even remember the passage of time. The treatment seemed to last for hours and transitioned into her telling me stories from Hawaiian history and from her practice.

She told me that after she retired from the massage-therapy practice at the Royal Hawaiian, she focused on consulting with other healers on difficult cases and on exorcisms of destructive spirit entities. One story she told me concerned a couple whose one-year-old son was gradually dying, losing his life force because of some undiagnosed illness. Tuning in with the infant's higher self, Morrnah saw that he needed something from the sea. She told the father to walk with his son into the ocean and let his son guide him. The father waded into the water up to his chest, holding his son until the infant reached out for a particular kind of floating seaweed. The parents took the seaweed, cooked it, and gave it to the son, who was cured.

Morrnah also told me a story about being consulted by a Japanese family in Hawaii who had experienced a series of violent deaths by accident or crime. Using her clairvoyant perception to tune in to the family's ancestral lineage, Morrnah saw that two or three generations previously in Japan, it included a samurai who had killed dozens of people. The traditional reverence for ancestors was unconsciously preserving the karma of this killer as a destructive presence in the life of the family. Morrnah contacted the soul of this long-deceased samurai and persuaded him to move upward, following the lines of light into the spirit world. The family was counseled to distinguish familial respect for the ancestor from personal approval of his deeds. They were thereby released from this lethal karmic possession that had been kept in place, inadvertently, by their reverence for the ancestors.

Morrnah also told me about an incredible series of exorcisms and karmic healings she had undertaken on behalf of the Hawaiian royal family and by extension the whole kingdom. She said she had realized that the practice of cannibalism in the kingdom in former centuries had left a karmic indebtedness that needed to be neutralized and exorcised, which she proceeded to do in a systematic manner. I do not know if she talked or wrote about this aspect of her work in later times. Her Wikipedia entry does not mention it, though it does talk about the rituals of *ho'oponopono*.

> In 1976 she began to modify the traditional Hawaiian forgiveness and reconciliation process of *ho'oponopono* to the realities of the modern day. Her version of ho'oponopono was influenced by her Christian (Protestant and Catholic) education and her philosophical studies about India, China and Edgar Cayce. The combination of Hawaiian traditions, praying to the Divine Creator, and connecting problems with reincarnation and karma resulted in a unique new problem solving process, that was self-help rather than the traditional Hawaiian group process. Her system uses *ho'oponopono* techniques to create a working partnership among the three parts of the mind or self, which she calls by the Hawaiian names, as well as by the terms subconscious, conscious, and superconscious.

The Wikipedia article states that Morrna devoted her later years to spreading the *ho'oponopono* process through teaching and workshops in the United States and several other countries, including Germany, the Netherlands, Switzerland, France, and Japan. She founded Pacifica Seminars in the 1970s, and in 1980, The Foundation of I, Inc.

In an entry of the Congressional Record dated March 25, 1992, U.S. Senator Daniel Akaka (D-Hawaii) eulogized Morrnah Simeona and her personal and international healing ministry. "He noted she had learned that the original plaster cast of the cast-iron Statue of Freedom, which stands on top of the US Capitol, was being kept in storage. She raised $25,000 to refurbish and restore it, and as a result it was moved and placed on display in the Russell Senate Building."

When I visited Morrnah in the 1970s, I had really no idea of the international spiritual healing work that she was beginning to develop—and that she herself only hinted at in the stories that she was telling me. I will always be grateful for the gift of healing she provided to help me cope with the traumatic aftereffects of my son's death. And I am thankful for the inspiration her life and work have provided for the possibilities of collective healing and international peacemaking.

During my trip to Hawaii, I almost met with Willard Wannall (1921–2000), who is one of the outstanding UFO/ET contactees of modern times and who was living there at the time. When I was studying the *agni yoga* meditation techniques in the Actualism group, one of my fellow students had obtained a copy of Wannall's autobiographical book in manuscript form. This book, called *Wheels Within Wheels and Points Beyond,* which is still available on the internet but has never been published as a regular book.

In this book Wannall, who had either retired or been dismissed from the army for his interest in UFO sightings, describes how his physical body went through a prolonged period of extraordinary changes in sense perceptions and physical capabilities. He attributed these changes to practices he was being taught by ET beings with whom he was in regular contact. However, they resulted in his being committed to a mental institution and given psychiatric medications and electroshock therapy. In his book, he describes his experience of going through a series of progressive initiatory teachings provided by a very high alien being from Venus called Ashtar, who gave him a guided tour of the advanced civilization inhabiting that planet. He was told that although our science correctly describes the planet as inhospitable to life in the equatorial region because of its extreme temperature, the civilization exists at the more even-tempered polar regions.

Ashtar warned Wannall that he would appear progressively more catatonic to outside observers as his consciousness was withdrawn from the regular Earth dimension. In fact, after his guided tour through supradimensional and extraplanetary worlds, which he describes with extraordinary lucidity in his book, Wannall returned to the Earth dimension to find himself strapped to a leather board and about to receive another of a series of electroshock treatments. He quickly learned to make the necessary changes in his outward behavior so that he could be discharged from the hospital—"cured" of his catatonic condition.

I had read Wannall's account in typescript and was extremely interested in meeting him when I came to Hawaii, especially because there were many points of overlap with the esoteric teachings we were receiving in the Actualism school. I did talk with him on the phone before I left for Hawaii. I noticed (and had been told) that he tape-recorded every telephone conversation. He had become cautious to the point of paranoia as a result of the sometimes brutal treatment he had endured at the hands of the military for his involvement in ET research. But we were unable to find a time to meet. As with Morrnah Simeona, I learned much more about him and his interesting discoveries from the internet, which did not exist at the time of my visit.

My interest in ETs and UFOs seems to have been stimulated or reawakened at least once every decade. In the late 1960s, when I was living in Berkeley in Tim Leary's old house, having moved there from Millbrook, I had my first meeting with a contactee. A man in his thirties came to the house and wanted to tell his story of a life-changing encounter, which, he said, affected him as powerfully as psychedelic experiences had apparently affected us. But he had difficulty finding people who would take his story seriously. He proceeded to tell of see-ing a UFO land in a field, watching alien beings emerging, and eventually feeling the beings taking him into the ship. They showed him how they could shape the landscape of meadows and trees in different colors outside by painting it on a kind of transparent easel inside the ship.

This contact story, which takes a few minutes to describe, took him a couple of hours of enormous effort to relate. He had apparently been given a posthypnotic implant to forget the abduction and was only able to describe it with difficulty. His obvious distress and effort in relating this story made it impossible for me to dismiss his account as demented fantasies. I agreed with him that his experience was clearly an expansion of consciousness and worldview in ways that we did not and still do not understand. I later wished that we could have stayed in touch so that I could hear more of his story. But I do not remember his name and never heard from him again.

FOUR

AN ENCOUNTER WITH AYAHUASCA SORCERY

In November 1990 I had the good fortune to accompany a small expedition organized by a group called Botanical Preservation Corps (BPC) to the Ecuadorian rainforest to study cultural and ethnobotanical aspects of certain visionary plants, particularly the concoction known as ayahuasca. This was one of the first such expeditions by BPC, a group of medicinal and visionary plant enthusiasts from Northern California. In later years this group organized a series of conferences on entheogenic plants and fungi in Palenque, Chiapas, Mexico, which attracted hundreds of participants.

The leaders of our small expedition were Rob Montgomery, a botanist specializing in medicinal and psychoactive plants, and Bret Blosser, an anthropologist and ethnobotanist who studied indigenous healing practices in Central and South America. I had had at that time perhaps two or three experiences with ayahuasca, in a North American setting, thanks to my friendship and connection with Terence McKenna. I was interested in pursuing a deeper understanding of this remarkable visionary plant concoction and its use by indigenous Amazonian shamans and healers.

On this particular expedition, our group of about a dozen people had gathered in Quito, the capital of Ecuador—an amazing city of two million inhabitants, situated almost exactly on the equator at 9,350 feet above sea level. We hired a driver with a minibus to take us, via Archidona and Tena, to the remote Jatun Sacha Biological Research Station near the Rio Napo. From the mountainous highlands of Quito, we descended on winding roads to the rainforest lowlands, eight hundred feet above sea level, making rest stops at tiny villages along the way. A couple of times when we stopped by the side of the road, Rob Montgomery, the avid botanist and plant collector, would rush into the forest to collect specimens of some rare medicinal plant he'd identified. The trip took almost ten hours, and we arrived after dark in a pouring rainstorm. We carried our bags and food boxes up a steep, narrow, and muddy footpath. At the Jatun Sacha station, there were wooden cabins, where we had bunk beds with mosquito nets. We were all exhausted and stressed, both by the altitude changes and the rough discomfort of the bus trip.

The next day we were instructed to walk into the forest and then to separate and each spend an hour alone, sitting quietly, letting our senses expand into the forest ecosystem. Plant, animal, fungal, and microbial life was seething and simmering above, below, and all around us. After I settled on my little piece of ground near a footpath, I was surrounded on all sides by a seemingly impenetrable wall of green over a hundred feet high, dripping with moisture, exuding waves of varied exotic plant perfumes, some putrid, some sweet and almost erotic. More birds started to sing as the sun rose higher, casting patches of light on the forest floor. I was meditating on the formal analogies between the serpentine form of the vine, the mother serpent said to be the spirit of the ayahuasca medicine, and the serpentine coilings of the intestines, the organ where the medicine exerts its purgative action.

—◆—

I had been reading a book called *Sicuanga Runa* (1985) by Norman Whitten, an anthropologist at the University of Illinois who made a lifelong study of the indigenous religious and shamanic traditions of the Ecuadorian Amazon region. I learned that the spirit of the plants and the forest is described as *un hombrecillo vestido de verde,* "a little man dressed in green." This nickname reminded me of the little green elves, male and female, that I had seen on my ayahuasca trips in Northern California.

My account of those visions was published, along with those of about twenty other people in a book I edited: *The Ayahuasca Experience* (2014). In that book I used the pseudonym Raoul Adamson for my own account, which was titled "Initiation into an Ancient Lineage of Visionary Healers."

> The ayahuasca jungle elves, the little green guys, are carrying away what look like armor plates and metallic pieces. I get the sense they are taking apart pieces of a structure, to wash and polish them and tune them up for better functioning. Suddenly I realize the structure they are dismantling is my *self.* I yell after them, inwardly, "hey, wait, that's *me* you're carrying away there". Without missing a beat, they reply cheerfully, "not to worry, we'll put you back together, you'll be fine". All the time they are singing in the rhythmic chants of the *icaros* sung by the guide. I had experienced, and heard of, shamanic dismemberment experiences before, where you are pounded and pulverized, or sliced and cut up, as a prelude to eventual healing reconstitution. But this was the first time I experienced this kind of civilized, courteous, efficient dismantling. The green elves were taking apart my character armor, and giving me back an improved, more flexible, more comfortable body-mind-system. (Metzner 2014, 121–2)

At the time of our expedition in Ecuador, I had had only two or three ayahuasca experiences, like the one cited above, mostly in the company of my friend Terence McKenna. They had been unreservedly positive, sometimes accompanied with intimate healing insights and transformations. I had not had any ayahuasca experiences with indigenous guides or shamans, as we were planning to have in our jungle encampment, but my attitude, though naïve, was confident and filled with positive anticipation. This turned out to be an important factor in helping me deal with the unexpected onslaught I was about to face.

We met with a local woman named Mercedes Mamayallacta, whose father was a Quechua *yachaj* (shaman healer). She told us how the initiation of a *yachaj* involves meeting Sacha Runa, the man (*runa*) of the forest (*sacha*), who invites you to his house in the forest, where you sit on a bench, which turns out to be an anaconda, while he teaches you about the plants and the animals. Actually, Sacha Runa is said to be a couple: men shamans are taught by the female, women by the male. (This practice reminded me of tantric initiatory traditions of India and Tibet I had heard about.) The *yachaj* work with ayahuasca, as well as with *guantu*—a *Brugmansia* species with properties similar to datura—and with tobacco, which is the most widely used psychoactive plant in indigenous South America. The *curanderos,* who work with other medicinal plants and herbs, are a separate profession.

Fig. 4.1. Ayahuasca being brewed, Ecuador, 1990. Photo by Bret Blosser

Fig. 4.2. Jungle camp meeting, Ecuador, 1990. Ralph Metzner is standing at left.
Photo by Bret Blosser

Rob Montgomery showed us the nursery of native medicinal plants he had been helping to build at the research station. Bret Blosser and David Neill, the botanist in charge of the Jatun Sacha station, gave talks on tropical rainforest ecology, with its intricate symbiotic webs, involving both competition and cooperation among plants, insects, birds, and mammals in a region that has the highest diversity of species on Earth. A local herbal *curandero* came and showed us how they prepare *guantu*. We were told that the Quechua shamans use it sparingly, separately from ayahuasca, for divining future situations as well as engendering premonitory dreams and finding lost objects.

That evening I decided to try a small amount of the *guantu*, although daytime use is considered preferable. I entered into a kind of floating trance between sleep and waking, a state some call *twilight sleep:* although the body is totally relaxed and still, you remain aware of the room you're in. For a brief time I had a sensation of flying around the camp, amid vague images of other sleepers, before I drifted off into deeper sleep.

In the morning I recalled two dreams: one was of a minor argument with my spouse, which turned out to be prophetic of a situation that would happen after my return. The other dream was of an unpleasant dispute with a colleague, which I took to be a warning not to engage in a possible collaborative project we had been discussing. The following evening, I again took a small amount of the *guantu* juice and dreamed of listening to a Hispanic woman giving a lecture on medicinal plants. This turned out to be a preview of Rocío Alarcón, an Ecuadorian woman plant healer who was scheduled to arrive the following day to talk to our group. Nothing in those dream visions, however, prepared me for what was to come.

That evening an ayahuasca session was arranged for our group with a local shaman whom I shall call Don Pablo (not his real name). We were driven in a truck for about twenty minutes until we arrived at

Fig. 4.3. Rob Montgomery, with local practitioner preparing brew.
Photo by Bret Blosser

his house, which stood on an elevated wooden platform in a cleared field. We climbed up a stepladder and were directed to sit on the floor in a circle, crowded together in almost total darkness. Don Pablo and his wife passed out little thimble-sized cups with the liquid. I was surprised, because this was a much smaller amount than I'd ever taken before—even though I knew potencies of ayahuasca could obviously vary. We were also told to keep smoking the strong *mapucho* tobacco, which is normally used in conjunction with ayahuasca almost everywhere in Amazonia.

Don Pablo started chanting in a raspy voice, with a repetitive descending phrase, that sounded totally unlike the soothing, lilting *icaros* that I had heard *ayahuasqueros* singing on recordings made by my friend the Colombian anthropologist Luis Eduardo Luna. I experienced a mild and pleasant sense of buoyancy and well-being, but no visions or healing insights with the characteristic purging. After about two hours I felt bored and uncomfortable in the crowded space, and had just about decided I was going to leave and climb down the stairs, when Don Pablo's wife announced that the session was over and we should all leave.

On the drive back to our camp, the discussion was one of bemused perplexity: Rob, Bret, and I had experienced ayahuasca before, and we assured the others, who were novices, that this was not the real thing. For some reason he had either not made the tea correctly or in enough quantity. Some of us felt we had been ripped off, since an amount of money had been paid to the shaman. I was puzzled and a bit disappointed, but not otherwise greatly disturbed. Rob and Bret determined that Don Pablo didn't brew the required mixture properly, either because he didn't know how or for some other reason. When corresponding later about this event, Rob mentioned that he recalled Don Pablo telling us before we started that one had to be watchful all the time for other evil *ayahuasqueros* and their bad spirits. A session with another *ayahuasquero*, Don Jaime, was arranged for the following day, through contacts made by Rocío Alarcón.

The night after we returned from our session with Don Pablo, I started shivering and shaking. By the next morning I was feverish, with a strong headache, constant shivering and shaking, weakness, and no appetite. I started to feel afraid for my safety and for my family. I drank water repeatedly, but just as often would retch it up. I had a homeopathic emergency kit with me, with a little printed guide to the remedies. I couldn't visually focus on the small print of the guide, so I asked Bret to find the remedy that best matched the symptoms I related to him. He picked out *Gelsemium* (yellow jasmine), for which the indications were listed as "flu-like symptoms with lethargy, weakness, achiness, shivering, occipital headache. No thirst. Body feels heavy and tired. Worse from dampness." I took some, at the 20c concentration I had, every couple of hours. The homeopathic physician I consulted later told me that was also the remedy he would have recommended.

That evening, our group assembled for the second ayahuasca session conducted by Don Jaime. I was far too sick by this time to ingest anything. As the ceremony started, Don Jaime had me sit in front of him, while he chanted, shook his dried-leaf rattle in a circle around my body, blew tobacco smoke at and around me, and did some sucking extraction from the top of my head. His *icaros* were very soothing—completely different from the raspy chants we had heard from Don Pablo. My feverish shivering stopped during his ministrations, only to resume when he stopped singing. That night and the following day, I laid in my bunk bed under mosquito netting, while someone checked in with me every hour or so, taking my temperature, which was rising. I was in a delirious fever state, with nonstop shaking. Every fifteen minutes or so I would drag myself outside to retch what was by now only fluid. Thoughts and images in glaring colors and jagged shapes were rushing chaotically through my head in a meaningless jumble. They felt so violent and intrusive that I was reluctant to close my eyes. I was afraid and slept fitfully, if at all.

The feverish delirium continued into the next day, with profound weakness, continuous shivering, and aching all over the body. I felt as if

I had been invaded by some unknown malignant force. It was obvious to all that I was getting seriously dehydrated. When I drank water, it tasted dry in my throat, and shortly afterward I would vomit liquid. In the afternoon, Don Jaime did another rattling and tobacco-smoke treatment, which gave me some relief. I was told it was Thanksgiving Day in the United States, but that fact barely registered in my consciousness. I did not feel celebratory.

The following day, since my condition was not improving, it was decided I needed to be evacuated to a hospital to get rehydrated. It was the planned last day of our trip, and the rest of the group went on a canoe trip. We agreed to meet up later in Quito for the return flight to the United States. Rocío Alarcón and two friends of hers drove me to a small hospital in Tena, where I was given intravenous infusions of saline, as is done with dehydrated infants. I had been without sleep, food, or water for three days. With sleep medication I finally found some rest and relief from the constant shaking and retching. I do not remember much of the return car trip to Quito or the return flight

Fig. 4.5. Ralph being whisked by Don Jaime during his sickness. Photo by Rob Montgomery

to San Francisco, except that I had to be taken aboard the plane in a wheelchair.

In writing up this story about twenty years later, I consulted with Bret Blosser and Rob Montgomery, to refresh my memory. Rob wrote: "When I caught up with you in Quito, you were really out of body and it took a bit to round up your stuff for the imminent flight home. The whole time I'm thinking to myself how (your wife) Cathy would never forgive me for letting you die. Somehow I got the airline with airport transfer points set up so there would be a wheelchair provided at every stop. I was not able to find your boots, so you went off in stocking feet. I'm sorry about that. I got your boots delivered by another participant later on."

After my return I went to see our allopathic family doctor, Milton Estes, M.D., who took blood samples and sent them to be tested. I also visited Jonathan Shore, M.D., the very experienced homeopathic physician I had been working with for some time, who prescribed a remedy based on my symptoms. Within a day or two I began to improve, and my energy level went up to 50 percent of normal, from less than 10 percent. I started to feel that I was on a path of healing and recovery.

Three days after my return, I was lying in my bed in Sonoma, drifting off to sleep. It was a moonlit night, and a profoundly peaceful feeling pervaded my awareness. I saw two small figurines, maybe a foot or so in height, a man and a woman, like Kachina dolls, except alive, on the window ledge. They were beaming at me, emanating benevolence and protection. Then it dawned on me: this was the Sacha Runa pair, the guardian spirits of the rainforest. They were reaching out to me from their faraway forest home, making sure that I was OK, and conveying regret that I had such a painful experience while in their realm. I was deeply touched.

Over the next several weeks, my healing process continued, supported by the homeopathic remedies. Test results having ruled out hepatitis and other common infections, six weeks after my return Dr. Estes told me that a laboratory specializing in tropical diseases had identified the illness as dengue fever. Dengue fever is a viral infection vectored by a mosquito bite. Also known as "bone-break," because of the violent feverish shaking and aching it causes, it can progress to more severe levels involving internal bleeding and death. There is no known cure, I was informed, but by the time I received that pessimistic prognosis, I was already cured. While there were certainly plenty of mosquitos around during our stay, I did not remember any particular insect bite preceding my fever.

I began to wonder whether I had been subjected to some kind of spirit attack. In the literature on South American indigenous and mestizo *curanderismo,* particularly in relation to ayahuasca, I found that harmful attacks by malevolent practitioners using invisible "darts" are widely reported. Perhaps as many as 50 percent of illnesses are said to be caused by such sorcery. The biography of Peruvian artist Pablo Amaringo by Luis Eduardo Luna gives dramatic accounts of these practices and their sometimes fatal consequences.

I was not so ideologically committed to the Western materialist worldview that I would discount such reports as impossible. I was well aware that negatively charged thought-forms, directed at others with focused intent can have devastating consequences. Envy among competitive health professionals, said to be the prime motivation for such attacks in South America, is well known in North America too, where it may manifest in malicious rumors and lawsuits, the slandering of reputations, and ruinous financial manipulations. Nor do I mean to single out doctors: malevolent envy and backbiting occur in all professions, including academia.

I remembered that Don Pablo, the first shaman we visited, had said that he spent two hours, before we started, "checking out the perimeter" of the field in which his house stood. I certainly had sympathy for his possible reluctance to give us a higher dose—a dozen inexperienced gringos, whacked out on ayahuasca on an elevated platform, could have spelled big trouble for him.

Later in December of that year, when I was at a retreat in the Southern California desert near Joshua Tree National Park, a couple of other possibilities occurred to me. One was that the attack came from Don Pablo himself; another was that it came from enemies of his, so that I would have been the victim of a kind of drive-by shooting. I realized that we knew nothing about his possible rivalries with other shamanic practitioners. He had lost a source of income when our group went to another healer after him. What did we know about the relationship between them? In my delirious state at the time, I didn't have the energy to inquire with Don Jaime, the second practitioner, about such factors. But I remembered my disappointment with Don Pablo's medicine, my dislike of his raspy chanting, and his cold, dismissive energy.

During that same desert vision retreat I also thought that probably my previous work with the healing spiritual energies of ayahuasca, and the bond I had made with the Serpent Mother Spirit (*Sachamama*) of the vine and the forest enabled me to survive the attack. Don Jaime's healing chants may have reinforced the connection to the Sacha Runa couple, who came to visit me after I had returned home to California.

In connection with the serpent spirit, it was interesting that from the three-day delirium of jumbled racing thoughts and images, the one and only word that I recalled was *Nagarjuna*. This was the name of a legendary second-century Indian Buddhist yogic adept and philosopher, and it means "White Serpent." (Nagarjuna was said to have been esoterically instructed by *nagas*—serpents.) He is regarded as the founder and prime exponent of the Madhyamika school—teaching the Middle Way of nonattachment to any concepts of reality. The ayahuasca serpent spirits may have been reminding me of nonattachment in that experience in the forest.

Some time after my return, my friends and fellow shamanic explorers Michael Harner and Sandra Ingerman came to visit. I told them about my experience and the questions I had been considering about the possible role of sorcery in my illness. Michael commented that it was always a good idea, when going into an environment with other shamanic practitioners, to fortify oneself with protective shields. I realized in retrospect that my attitude in going into the Ecuadorian rainforest to take ayahuasca with persons unknown to me had been quite naïve. My mind-set toward taking hallucinogens had been formed first in the easygoing 1960s and later by California New Age practices of taking psychoactive substances with trusted therapists and friends. There was an element of nondiscernment and overidealizing of indigenous people and their practices in my attitude.

In relation to my question about whether I was a bystander victim of a rivalry between healers or a target myself, Michael Harner also commented that perhaps I had been singled out because, with my gray hair, I was seen as the eldest and most experienced person in the group. It was the old gang-fighting principle of attacking the leader first. A delightful synchronicity occurred while the three of us were sitting in my living room discussing these thorny issues of malice and evil. My two-year-old daughter Sophia came running down the hallway, stark naked, shrieking with laughter while waving a black plastic devil's stick left over from the last Halloween.

So the question of whether my bout with dengue fever was the consequence of an unfortunate but random encounter with a virus-vectoring mosquito, or whether the mosquito sting was the materialized dart of a malicious, ill-mannered *yachaj,* was left unresolved in my mind and remains so to this day. However, an unexpected postscript occurred eleven years later, which lent additional weight to the second possibility and the sorcery factor.

In May 2001 I attended and spoke at a conference on entheobotany, organized by the successor organization to the Botanical Preservation Corps, in Whistler, near Vancouver, British Columbia. Rocío Alarcón, an ethnobotanist associated with Ecoscientia, a conservation institute in Ecuador, also spoke at this conference, presenting her research on the medicinal uses of the ayahuasca vine and other herbal preparations. For the first time since the experience eleven years before, I had the opportunity to speak with her about it. She told me that she knew Don Jaime, the second shaman we worked with—in fact she had made the contact with him to work with our group. She said that when Don Jaime heard that we were going to do an ayahuasca session with Don Pablo, he had warned her that the latter had an unsavory reputation, and they were both concerned that someone in our group might get sick. So her testimony reinforced the idea that I was a deliberate target in the attack, not just an accidental victim.

The conversation with Rocío represented closure for me—to a fascinating cycle of shamanic sickness, dismemberment, sorcery, initiation, and healing. I don't regret any of it. I am grateful to Rocío for her witnessing and support, to Don Jaime for his healing, to Michael Harner for his counsel and his insights, to Bret and Rob for their companionship and friendship, to the great Serpent Mother of the visionary vine for her lessons in nonattachment, and to Sacha Runa, the Forest Elder Spirits, for their benevolence and compassion.

FIVE

CONVERSATIONS WITH ALBERT HOFMANN, MASTER ALCHEMIST

Albert Hofmann's discovery of LSD, the most potent mind-expanding substance ever found, was an event with multiple synchronicities. It occurred in 1943, at the height of World War II, within months of the building of the first atomic bomb—as if it was to be a kind of healing antidote to the mass death weapon that had just been invented and was shortly to be unleashed upon the world. The discovery occurred in Switzerland, a country with a seven-hundred-year history of political neutrality and with a centuries-long tradition of alchemy, which is the psychospiritual countercurrent to reductionistic materialist science. It involved a previously unknown substance that could induce integrative expansions of awareness, with profound implications for healing, for creative problem solving, and for cosmological understanding. Albert Hofmann had the scientific and the spiritual insight to recognize the enormous significance of his discovery and spent the rest of his long life (1906–2008) exploring it with an ever-widening international circle of collaborating scientists, artists, and visionaries.

In 1968, when I had separated myself from the Harvard group of psychedelic researchers and was working as a psychotherapist at Mendocino State Hospital in Northern California, I wrote an essay called "On the Evolutionary Significance of Psychedelics," which was published in an obscure journal called *Main Currents in Modern Thought*. Summarizing my reflections after five years of involvement in various research projects, I suggested that the effects of substances like LSD could be considered in the context of the evolution of consciousness.

If LSD expands consciousness and if, as is widely believed, further evolution will take the form of an increase in consciousness, then can we not regard LSD as a possible *evolutionary instrument*? Here is a substance which, by altering the chemical composition of the cerebro-sensory information processing medium, temporarily inactivates the screening programs, the genetic and cultural filters which dominate in a completely unnoticed way our usual perceptions of the world. (Metzner 1968, 24)

I had corresponded with Albert Hofmann, asking him to contribute an article for *The Psychedelic Review,* a quarterly journal published by the Harvard project of which I was one of the three editors. I continued to edit and publish this journal throughout the sixties and early seventies, at first while we were still at Harvard and later when I was living in Millbrook, then in New York City and then Berkeley, after migrating to California in the mid-1970s. During the later 1960s and early 1970s, my relationship with psychedelic research and the associated underground culture was increasingly distant, as psychedelics were made illegal and socially stigmatized.

My first personal meeting with Albert Hofmann occurred in 1977, in connection with a conference in San Francisco on hallucinogenic mushrooms at which we both spoke. We met at a reception in the Fitz Hugh Ludlow Memorial Library, which was established in that city to preserve scientific, ethnographic, and personal literature on hallucinogenic plants, fungi, and drugs.

I had received a postdoctoral research fellowship, during which I took the second-year pharmacology course at the Harvard Medical

School and wrote a long review of what was known of the chemistry and pharmacology of psychedelic drugs at that time. My knowledge of chemistry and pharmacology was purely text-based; I was a psychologist by training. So here was the psychologist meeting the master chemist who was my scientific hero for his groundbreaking discoveries. In the photo below, I am talking with Albert and Michael Horowitz, one of the library's founders. Hofmann was seventy-one, and I was forty-one. Over the next twenty-four years we continued to meet at least once or twice a year, most often in Europe, at his home in Switzerland, or at various conferences. Hofmann became for me, as he was for so many, an inspiring model of a visionary mystic as well as an impeccable scientist.

A few years later, in 1979, Hofmann's autobiographical account of the discovery of LSD appeared, entitled *LSD: Mein Sorgenkind.* This appeared in English translation as *LSD: My Problem Child.* The German word *Sorgenkind,* however, means a child (*Kind*) about whom you have care and concern (*Sorgen*), which has a slightly different con-

Fig. 5.1. Ralph Metzner (left) and Albert Hofmann (right) with Michael Horowitz at the opening ceremony of the Fitz Hugh Ludlow Memorial Library in San Francisco in 1977. Hofmann is holding Metzner's book *The Ecstatic Adventure.*
Photo by Michael Aldrich

notation than "problem child." Throughout his life Hofmann never referred to LSD as his invention but rather as his discovery. Strange though it may seem, I sometimes heard him say, that "LSD found me." It was as if the spirit behind this magical substance that has had such a profoundly positive impact on human consciousness and culture chose him to be the one to bring it through into material form under the auspices of a Swiss pharmaceutical company.

In 1983, when MDMA (later known as Ecstasy) was first becoming known and explored, some meetings were organized at the Esalen Institute in Big Sur, California, by Stanislav Grof, M.D., who was at that time a Resident Fellow there. The purpose of these meetings was to explore and discuss the nature and the potentials of this new substance, which was still legal at that time, both as an aid to psychotherapy and for consciousness research. About two dozen researchers and explorers gathered for two weeks of talks and discussions, which naturally also included some personal experimentation. I had by that time started to use the term *empathogenic* to describe the effect of MDMA, to distinguish it from the classical hallucinogens. This substance seemed to induce a state of nonverbal empathic connection with others, which is so essential in psychotherapy, but without the spectacular visual or auditory phantasmagoria characteristic of the classical hallucinogens.

In one of our group conversations during these sessions, Albert said, "With this substance, matter and mind are one," which seemed to summarize the essential simplicity and grounded goodness of the MDMA experience. A while later, as I was reflecting on the astonishing discoveries he had made in his work with natural substances, I said, "Nature reveals her deepest and most beautiful secrets to those who love her," and Albert pressed my hand in silent affirmation. In January 1984 I received a letter from him with a photo of his mountain home in Rittimatte, in the Alps near the border between Switzerland and France. He wrote, "I am happy to collaborate with you and our California friends in order to help people open their eyes and minds for the message of the Creation, its beauty and wonder."

In 1989 I received a letter from Albert in which he thanked me for sending him my most recently published book. It was the German translation of my book originally called *Opening to Inner Light,* which was subsequently republished in a new edition as *The Unfolding Self.* In it I describe ten major metaphors of the spiritual transformation at the core of spirituality and religion. In his letter, Albert described his reflections: "How did it come to the Babylonian 'confusion of tongues', which is expressed in the fragmentation of consciousness? I think that this fundamental question can only be answered if we keep in mind that the archetypes, the fundamental metaphors, are symbols for the fundamental structures of reality—but not the reality itself. There is only one objective reality (*Wirklichkeit*). We may hope that increasingly human beings will search for direct access to the source—the first-hand revelation. This will lead to humanity becoming more unified in its perceptions of reality (*Wirklichkeitsbewusstseins*) and to more cosmic consciousness as well." Albert also sent me a copy of his recently published book *Insight and Outlook*—a little jewel of wisdom sayings.

In March 1990, I received a letter from Albert in which he thanked me for my contribution to a Festschrift in his honor. The German title of the volume was *Das Tor zu inneren Räumen* (published in English as *Gateway to Inner Space).* The editor was our mutual friend, the German anthropologist Christian Rätsch. Albert wrote, "It is probably unnecessary that I describe in detail how much I concur with your thoughts and views. We have both drunk from the same source." In my essay in that volume, entitled "Molecular Mysticism: The Role of Psychoactive Plants in the Transformation of Consciousness," I emphasized that one cannot describe or evaluate the effects of a psychoactive plant or substance separately from the intention, or set and setting, with which it is used. Experiences with the same substance can range from sacramental to the therapeutic to the recreational, or even to the maliciously disorienting, according to the set—that is, the mind-set.

I had suggested in that essay that one could think of psychedelics as "gnostic catalysts." *Gnosis* is the ancient term for sacred knowledge

Fig. 5.2. Albert Hofmann's ninetieth birthday party, at Rittematte, 1996. From left to right: Christian Rode, Rolf Verres, Hofmann, Peter Gasser, and Ralph Metzner. Photo by Chris Heidrich

or insight into the fundamental realities of the universe. I also wrote that the term *entheogen*, which some colleagues were beginning to use instead of *psychedelic*, was an "unfortunate choice in a way, since it suggested that the divine (*theos*) was somehow being generated (*gen*) in these states, with these substances. My own experiences have rather led me to the opposite conclusion—that the divine within *is* the creator, the source of life-energy, the power to awaken and to heal." In his letter Albert wrote: "I agree completely with your critical considerations on the use of the term *entheogen*. The concept of a catalyst on the other hand is probably more readily understandable to a chemist than a non-chemist." I eventually reconciled myself to the use of the term *entheogen*, because it is the only one that explicitly refers to the spiritual dimensions of the experience.

In 1996, Albert and I crossed paths again in the context of a conference at the University of Heidelberg, organized by Dr. Rolf Verres, director of the Psychosomatic Clinic at the university, and his wife, Dörthe. During this conference there was a wonderful dinner party organized by the Verres family, in which Charles Grob, Rick Doblin, and Juraj and Sonja Styk also participated. Albert, who was by this time enjoying his retirement from his professional position at Sandoz Pharmaceuticals, was in great form, regaling everyone with his stories.

One of the participants at this party was a judge from the North German town of Lübeck, Wolfgang Neskovic, who had just successfully pleaded a case before the German Federal Constitutional Court. He argued that, as a matter of fundamental jurisprudence, a drug or substance could not be declared illegal per se; only the human behavior associated with a drug could be illegal. This judgment eventually led to a domino effect in the various German states, each passing laws regulating the quantities of cannabis that could be legally purchased and used.

A couple of years later, in December 1998 and January 1999, I exchanged letters with Albert in which we referred to conversations we had had with a number of other colleagues at a symposium called "Psychedelic Elders" in Kalamazoo, Michigan, that was organized by the Institute of Noetic Sciences and the Fetzer Institute. In this gathering Albert, who had turned ninety in 1996, was the honored elder. After the meetings I wrote a letter to him expressing some concern that perhaps there had been a misunderstanding between us. There had been lively discussions about the relative advantages and disadvantages of psychoactive plants and fungi versus pharmaceutical drug preparations. As I remember, I had expressed the opinion—which I know is shared by many researchers, including my friend and colleague Andrew Weil— that natural plants and fungi may be safer for human use because the "medicine" is not so concentrated. I had written, in my letter to Albert Hofmann:

> As Paracelsus had said, "The difference between the medicine and the poison is in the dosage." Perhaps the plants and herbs are safer because the dosage is generally going to be lower whereas the con-

centrated drugs are more effective because the dosage is higher. In that case safety and effectiveness of a medicine are more a matter of attitude, knowledge, consciousness and use. What is your view on this question?

In his letter Hofmann, the old master, replied:

The essential difference between the purified substance and the botanical preparation (whether whole plant or extract) is that the dosages in the former can be more precisely calibrated than in the plant preparations. This is particularly important with those substances in which the difference between an effective dose and a lethal dose is small (the so-called *therapeutic breadth*). With heroin, for example, the therapeutic breadth is very low—1:3. This means that a dose only three times higher than the normal effective dose can kill you. This is the reason why there are so many heroin over-dose deaths. With LSD the therapeutic breadth is very large. The exact figure is not known, since there have never been any cases of death attributable to the physical effect of LSD. The danger with LSD consists of the depth of the psychological effect—if the experience cannot be integrated and leads to psychic disturbances and associated catastrophic actions. Thus, despite the very wide therapeutic breadth, the precise calculation of dosages of LSD is of the utmost importance.

In 2006 Albert Hofmann turned one hundred years old, and there were multiple celebrations and publications in his honor, including an address by the president of the Swiss Federation. Many people have felt that he should have been awarded the Nobel Prize in chemistry for his many discoveries in that field (in addition to LSD), but the Nobel committee apparently felt that this work was too controversial. In any case, the Swiss public and the international scientific community felt no such constraints, and his hundredth birthday celebration drew two thousand people and hundreds of media representatives from all over the world.

Festschrift volumes, both in English and German, had been prepared for this occasion, containing essays by friends and colleagues recognizing, extending, and illustrating the insights behind Albert's discoveries. In one such publication I published an essay entitled "The Quest for the Alchemical Philosopher's Stone." It was later reprinted as the prologue to my book *Ecology of Consciousness* (2017).

In this essay I described how the transformational teachings of alchemy, originating in the sacred science of ancient Egypt, persecuted by the church in the Middle Ages, and ridiculed by scientific modernism, were a "lost science." Alchemy existed long before the conceptual split between matter and spirit that occurred with the rise of materialistic science from the sixteenth century onward. Its knowledge was then submerged, but was revived in the twentieth century by the work of two Swiss scientist-scholars: C. G. Jung, who identified alchemical symbolism as the objective language of the psyche, and Albert Hofmann, whose discovery of LSD reconnected the broken link between spirit and matter—the mysterious link traditionally known as the *philosophers' stone*. I made my argument by taking some of the bafflingly obscure and mysterious statements of the alchemists and showing how they could apply to experiences triggered by psychedelic substances. I concluded by writing:

> I am *not* saying that LSD or any other psychoactive molecule *is* the legendary Stone of the Philosophers. I am saying that through the discovery of psychedelic substances, and in particular LSD (with its extremely high potency), and in his recognition of its spiritual significance, Albert Hofmann re-connected the broken thread of the West's alchemical wisdom tradition. In making his contributions to published scientific chemistry and medicine, at the time and the place in which he found himself, he provided all present and future seekers a wonderful aid in their quest for that most precious Wisdom Water-Stone, and a key to liberating self-knowledge. For

that, I bow to Albert Hofmann, from the depths of my soul, with the most profound gratitude.

Albert later told me how much that essay meant to him—since he was unfamiliar with the rich and deep teachings of alchemy. As a scientist in the Western materialist tradition but also as a man with deep spiritual and mystical leanings, he appreciated knowing of these older wisdom teachings.

I visited Albert in his mountain home in Rittimatte each summer in the last three years of his life, in the company of Roger Liggenstorfer, Chris Heidrich, Christian Rode, and other friends and colleagues. All of us remarked how clear he still was and how strong his voice was, without quavering or trembling. I cherish the memory of these visits, when Albert and his wife, Anita, would receive us with tea and cake, and with the plum liqueur that he had made. Wonderful free-flowing conversations ensued as we sat in the golden light of the afternoon sun setting over the Jura Mountains. When I arrived with my friends in 1996, Albert had received and read my essay, and he welcomed me at the door of his house, saying, "Instead of bowing to me, let us embrace."

On my last visit with Albert in 2007, when he was 101, we had what was for me a most memorable conversation. I had found out that St. Anthony's Fire (German: *Antoniusfeuer*) was one of the colloquial names of a viral skin infection known as *shingles* in English or *Gürtelrose* in German. This disease is caused by an infestation of the herpes zoster virus in the nerves of the skin, causing reddish, blistering eruptions, often around the middle of the body (whence the German name, which means "belt rose"). It can also infect the nerves in the face—around the eyes, ears, cheek, and so on—usually on one side. The disease is treated in modern medicine with antiviral drugs, but is notorious for its unrelenting painfulness. I experienced this infection in my facial nerves in the 1990s and can confirm that the pain never stops and the affected nerves never stop screaming "fire" until the infection has run its course.

Now it so happens that St. Anthony's Fire is also a name for a different toxic disease—ergot poisoning. Ergot (German: *Mutterkorn*) is the name of a fungus, *Claviceps purpurea,* that infects rye and other cereal grasses. Eating cereal grasses or bread contaminated with ergot is believed to have caused epidemics of ergotism in the Middle Ages. Symptoms of ergot poisoning include painful seizures and spasms, paresthesia, gangrene of the fingers and toes, itching, possible hallucinations, and eventual death. According to Wikipedia, St. Anthony's Fire, also known historically as *ignis sacer* or *holy fire,* was the name commonly used for ergotism in France and Germany, and for the herpes zoster infection in Italy and Malta.

The question that arose in my mind was whether the libidinous and gruesome hallucinations, commonly interpreted as "temptations," that the fourth-century mystic Saint Anthony of Egypt was said to have endured during his long fasts in desert solitude—and the source of some of the most dramatic paintings in Western art—might have been induced, in part, by his eating of pieces of bread tainted by ergot, as well as by the herpes zoster virus. According to legend, his food intake for a long time was reduced to one piece of bread a month. As the story goes, Anthony did eventually overcome his demons and healed his skin afflictions. He emerged from his hermitage and spent the last thirty years of his life preaching and teaching. According to legend, he lived to the age of 103.

Albert Hofmann was a medicinal chemist working for the Sandoz company, isolating and identifying the chemical structure of traditional medicinal products for the pharmaceutical markets. His area of specialization was the chemistry of ergot alkaloids based on lysergic acid; and LSD is lysergic acid diethylamide. There was particular interest at Sandoz in ergot derivatives for their oxytocic effect—stimulating uterine contractions. Hofmann's lab produced the Sandoz pharmaceutical Methergine, which is still in use for stimulating contractions in childbirth. The application of ergot products in obstetrics was apparently known in the Middle Ages; hence the German name for ergot: *Mutterkorn* (mother grain). In Albert's circle of friends and colleagues, there was the half-serious suggestion that whereas other ergot derivatives stimulated uterine childbirth, the LSD-derivative stimulated spiritual rebirth.

In our conversation, I asked Albert about the paradox of a natural product, a parasitical fungus called ergot, which, in one form, was the source of a painful and potentially fatal nervous-system toxicosis, in another form the source of a beneficial obstetric medicine, and in still another derivative form a physically safe medicine that could induce visions of cosmic consciousness. How did medieval physicians and midwives distinguish between these three applications? His answer came back to the principle articulated by the great sixteenth-century physician Paracelsus—*the difference between the medicine and the poison is in the dosage.* The amount of lysergic-acid derivative involved in ergot

Fig. 5.3. Albert Hofmann (right) in 2006, at the age of one hundred, looking west into the Jura Mountains at sunset. From left to right: Ralph Metzner, Roger Liggenstorfer, Hofmann. Photo by Chris Heidrich

poisoning is substantial, whereas the ergot derivative in LSD is notorious for efficacy in an almost microscopic quantity.

When I told Albert about how the name St. Anthony's Fire is associated with shingles (which he did not know) as well as with ergot poisoning (which of course he did know), he was surprised and intrigued. He told me that St. Anthony was his patron saint. It is apparently not uncommon in Switzerland, which is predominantly a Protestant country, for people still to have a personal saint as an inspirational figure. I thought to myself, here is another one of those curious synchronicities: Anthony the desert hermit lived to the age of 103, Albert Hofmann to the age of 102!

Some well-meaning but overenthusiastic American admirers of Hofmann's contribution to their processes of enlightening consciousness have sometimes referred to him as "Saint Albert." I myself, and most of my European friends, were uncomfortable with this idealizing ten-

Fig. 5.4. Albert Hofmann (left) sitting with Ralph Metzner in 2006.
Photo by Chris Heidrich

dency and have told this to the people involved. I believe Albert was also uncomfortable with it, though he was much too courteous to say so.

Along these lines, I remember a conference at the University of California, Santa Cruz, in the mid-1970s, to which Albert Hofmann was invited. It was his first public conference appearance in the United States, and he was greeted with a thunderous standing ovation before he had said a word. He seemed slightly taken aback and said shyly, "I am only a chemist, not a guru." This was how he saw his contribution and his legacy in the world—not a guru and not a saint, but a scientist, humbly dedicated to the search for knowledge, and a mystic, inspired by his vision of the great mystery.

SIX

MEETING MR. IBOGAINE

In the mid-1960s I was introduced to a remarkable African hallucinogen known as *iboga* or *eboka*. It is used in the form of ground-up root bark of the *Tabernanthe iboga* plant, or as a semisynthetic powdered substance called *ibogaine*. Preparations made from the bark of the roots of this tropical shrub play a major role in the initiatory and healing rituals of the Bwiti cult in equatorial Africa (the countries Zaire, Gabon, and Congo). The death of the old self and rebirth of a new and healthier self are the underlying themes of these rituals, which involve consuming enormous quantities of a mush containing the ground-up roots of this plant. The iboga rituals may be organized as transition initiations, for example for adolescents; or they may be curative ceremonies for various psychic and physical conditions. The ceremonies can go on for several hours or for as long as three days and can involve an extended family or a whole village. The initiate is supported, bathed, and ceremonially painted by older members of the cult, while drummers, musicians, and dancers keep up a nonstop accompaniment.

Semisynthetic extracts of ibogaine were used as adjuncts to psychotherapy and for the treatment of addictions in the 1960s by Claudio Naranjo, Leo Zeff, Jack Downing, and some other psychotherapists, including me. The dosages used in these psychotherapeutic sessions in the 1960s were much lower than those currently used in centers in Mexico, Guatemala, and other places where drug addicts and alcoholics can go for detox and treatment. The sessions in such centers involve massive doses (several grams) of synthetic ibogaine and can last up to ten or twelve hours. They require close medical supervision because of the risk of fatality from this drug in the population of addicts. In our studies with this substance, the amount taken was much more moderate and induced experiences similar in duration and intensity to a moderate to high dose of LSD or mescaline—i.e., five to seven hours.

In our studies in the late 1960s and early 1970s, I was impressed by the potential of ibogaine-enhanced psychotherapy. In contrast to the classical kaleidoscopic imagery with personal associations and the roller coaster of emotions found with mescaline, LSD, or psilocybin, the ibogaine trip seemed to have an assertively objective yet totally nonjudgmental quality. In those early years, friends and colleagues of mine who were familiar with it referred to the spirit of this medicine as clearly adult and masculine, calling it "Mr. Ibogaine." This quality was in marked contrast to the serpentine female spirits of ayahuasca and the playful child spirits (*los niños*) associated with the Mexican magic mushroom. I also learned a lot about iboga and ibogaine from Giorgio Samorini, an Italian ethnobotanist and historian of culture who was one of the first Westerners to be initiated in the Bwiti cult in Gabon in the early 1960s.

In his writings Claudio Naranjo referred to ibogaine as the "drug of analysis," noting its cool, detached quality in contrast to the empathic warmth of MDA and MDMA experiences. This analytical attitude seems congruent with the application of ibogaine in treating addiction, where subjects report being able to self-analyze their compulsive behavior patterns while freed, even if temporarily, from the relentless pull of the addictive drug. Visions obtained with ibogaine are unlike the typical kaleidoscopic "retinal circus" that can occupy your eyeballs with mushrooms or LSD. They are more like scenes in a landscape some distance away, but they could be brought forward for a closer look, like adjusting the focal length of binoculars through which you are looking.

On a cool December day in 1972, in a country house in Northern

California, I met this African teaching plant for the first time, accompanied by my partner and another close friend. We each took two grams of a dry brown powder that had been rasped from the bark of the root of this shrub. It was almost two hours before we began to notice the first effects. For me, these were a kind of visual enhancement of the edges and contours of objects, accompanied by some tight sensations and pressure around my head. This head pressure continued more or less through the whole experience, becoming at times quite intense. I had read that the Fang people of Gabon, who use eboka in the Bwiti cult, say that this medicine "opens up your head," so that the ancestor spirits can come in and talk to you. At times, it felt as if the two halves of my skull were opening from the top and falling apart, like a cracked coconut shell.

Then I noticed that my short-term memory seemed to be disrupted, so that it became difficult to complete sentences or thoughts. I was inclined to attribute this loosening of concentration to the cannabis we were also smoking, but then I obtained an insight and an image about this effect that I've never had with cannabis. The image was that the thoughts I kept grasping at and losing were like paper ribbons streaming past and through my head. It seemed I was trying to grasp them with my hands, but they kept slipping through my fingers. Then I realized that I could intentionally hold on to only those thought streamers that were new and significant. I realized by this image how by the loosening of old and familiar associative patterns, my mind was being cleared for receiving and recognizing new connections and new insights.

I began to see visions of African people and children, village scenes with much activity—farming, working, dancing, singing, playing, laughing. The visions were subtle and muted, as if seen from a distance, not bright and in-your-face sparkling, like those of ayahuasca and mushrooms. After a while I noticed there were also one or two white-skinned children, dressed in European clothes, among the Africans. At first I wondered—how curious, what are they doing here in this African village? Then I realized—with a sudden jolt of self-awareness—that these were memory images from my own childhood, of myself and my family, mingled in with the African scenes.

I became aware of an image of my mother. I saw her head and upper torso as she appeared to me when I was a child; then as she looked to me when I was an adolescent, then as an adult, in my twenties, then in my thirties, and so on. These images flashed by in fairly rapid succession, almost like the scenes we see in a trailer for a film—extracts from a life story. Each image of my mother was part of a *gestalt,* a patterned perception that also included my thoughts, feelings, and attitudes at that time in my life. It was a highly condensed review of the essential features of my mother and myself in our relationship through various phases of my life. There was absolutely no guilt, blame, regret, shame, resentment, or self-judgment of any kind involved in this review. It was objective, detached, and calm, but not cold. The emotions involved in the relationship, both positive and negative, were all included in the observation, with the same blend of detached but compassionate understanding. I could see how valuable this kind of nonjudgmental life review would be for healing addictive and compulsive habit patterns.

Subsequently I went through similar reviews of my relationships with other significant figures—with my father, my siblings, friends, and lovers. I was immensely appreciative for this compassionate, nonjudgmental mirroring of my life. In prior self-examinations, whether in psychotherapy or even with other psychoactive medicines, I had never been able to totally escape from the endless cycles of regret, guilt, blame, and shame attached to the so-called shadow sides of my nature. But in this ibogaine state, I could look at these patterns and see them objectively for what they were—the thoughtlessness, the arrogance, the weakness, and so on—without collapsing into guilt, denial, or rationalization.

The objective attitude with which I regarded my own character manifestations was comparable to the objectivity with which I might regard my legs, my feet, my hands—a kind of "just so" attitude: "Yep, that's the way I am." It was humbling but without being humiliating as psychedelic journeys into the hell realms of self-judgment can be. I also saw brief scenarios of myself in various roles—the professor giving a lecture, the therapist, the father, the writer. I realized that this kind of detached yet compassionate life review was the key to the remarkable efficacy of ibogaine for the treatment of addictions: the suicidal load of guilt that typically afflicts addicts can be, at least temporarily, suspended.

After a couple of hours of this life review and character mirroring, I became aware that I was again, or still, observing the African village scene: I saw the thatched-roof huts, the trees and animals, the children playing and running, the adults walking or sitting, working or dancing, talking or singing—I was observing everything from a slight distance. As I was taking all this in, I suddenly found myself more in the center of the village, and standing in front of me was an older man, wearing a broad-brimmed hat that hid his face and holding a tall staff in his hand. He was wearing khaki shorts and was barefoot, and I could see his broad feet splayed out on the hard-packed earth.

Simultaneously, I got the thought that he was the "Ancestor" and also realized that he was looking directly at me. I realized, of course, that he couldn't literally be my ancestor, since I don't have any African genes. He was an archetypal ancestor and elder, and I accepted him as such without question. Facing me, he was making strange gestures with his hands, as if holding up pictures to show me. I was awe-struck as I realized that he was the one who had been showing me the memory images from my life! He was the Elder, the Truth-Speaker, the one who read the contents of my mind, and he was teaching me by mirroring. And although I have absolutely no genetic relationship to any Africans, I had connected with him through the sacred eboka plant, known as "the bridge to the ancestors."

Having definitely captured my attention, after a while this intriguing figure turned and walked away, surrounded by other adults and children, to whom he was talking and gesturing. I realized too that his broad-rimmed, face-hiding hat, and the staff he was carrying, immediately reminded me of that other ancestor-teacher from the Nordic tradition, the shamanic god Odin, with whom I have long had a strong connection. As the African Ancestor turned and walked among his people, the staff and hat disappeared and I realized that this guide-teacher had adopted features of the Nordic deity with whom I was familiar for my benefit—so I would recognize who he was and what he was doing! I was deeply moved with gratitude for the encounter with this ancestral African Teacher.

About ten years later, in the mid-1980s, I had the opportunity to share an ibogaine experience with my partner, Cathy, and some other people I was collaborating with at that time. We had discovered that we could obtain an alcohol-concentrated extract of ibogaine, called the "mother tincture," from a French homeopathic supply house. (The mother tincture is the original plant extract from which the highly diluted homeopathic remedies are prepared through successive dilutions and succussions.) Because we wanted to take the medicine as close to undiluted as possible, we took the mother tincture. It was in a 55 percent alcohol solution, like strong brandy, so it had to be sipped slowly and with lots of water to avoid alcohol intoxication.

In this session too, we found that awareness of the ibogaine effect came on gradually. At one point, as my other friend and I were describing what we were seeing, Cathy said, "Listening to you talk, I realize I too have been having a vision." Later, she wrote in her account: "I saw a big, billowy black woman coming down from the sky. She had a gorgeous, pronounced face with eyes full of fiery passion and bedevilment. Her long black hair swayed in the wind. First I saw a destructive aspect of her face, and then I saw the trickster aspect of her face. Her hair grew longer and thicker, and her body size increased as she traveled closer to the ground. Then I somehow realized that she was the Tornado Goddess." Her message to Cathy was that she was to assimilate all that she had been given—that it was basically one's responsibility, on receiving a gift, to fully assimilate it. Cathy was totally surprised by this vision, having no idea that there even was such a figure as a tornado goddess. Neither she nor I had any knowledge of African mythology or religion at this time.

However, a few days later I was in a bookstore, and a striking synchronicity occurred: my eyes happened to light upon a book, which neither Cathy nor I had seen before, called *Oya: In Praise of an African Goddess,* by Judith Gleason. The cover had the following description, which seemed to fit perfectly with Cathy's visionary experience of this deity.

> The black goddess Oya manifests in powerful forms of nature: the great river Niger, strong winds and tornadoes, lightning and fire. . . . The Yoruba associate her with funerals and with masquerades constructed of bulky, billowing cloth. . . . One may speak of Oya as patron of feminine leadership, of persuasive charm and magical powers. . . . More abstractly, Oya is the goddess of edges, of the dynamic interplay of surfaces, of transformation from one state of being to another. As such, she is a jittery goddess. Always vanishing, she presents herself in concealment.

From West Africa, the worship of Oya, along with that of the other *orixas* (spirits), was brought to Brazil by slaves, where they became incorporated in the Afro-Brazilian religious movements known as Candomblé and Umbanda. These cults in turn migrated to the Caribbean and the United States. Groups of devotees of Oya and cult practitioners can be found today in New York City, and probably also in New Orleans.

It was interesting to realize that although the African plant medicine had opened up, for Cathy, a connection to an African deity, it was a deity from West Africa (where eboka is not known or used) who had been transplanted to the New World. Oya was not a deity specifically associated with the iboga-using Bwiti cult. In my own experience, on the other hand, there was a vision of an ancestral spirit that is recognized as characteristic of the Bwiti religion, but it was mingled with features from my own ancestral European religious mythology. In my book *The Ayahuasca Experience* (2014), I relate the story of an American man, who, while taking the Amazonian plant medicine ayahuasca, unexpectedly found himself in the role of a priest in the ancient Egyptian cult of the goddess Sekhmet, of which he had absolutely no prior knowledge.

These stories illustrate that while visionary states induced by entheogenic medicines are sometimes, in some respects, related to the plants' geographical and cultural habitats, this is not always the case. We may be given access to what Jungians call the cultural unconscious, the culture-specific matrix of archetypal forms. At the same time we may find ourselves, regardless of personal origin, accessing the collective unconscious, the species-wide reservoir of mythic images that forms the ancestral treasure-house of all of humanity.

⎯ ⎯

During the time I was working with the ibogaine tincture in my exploratory divination groups, there were many experiences that mentioned this kind of connection both with familial ancestors as well as with the greater spirits of nature and those from other cultures. I include here two accounts from my friend Winston ("Wink") Franklin (1940–2004), one of the founders of the Institute of Noetic Sciences, who gave me permission to publish these stories in my writing on ibogaine. In the first account, he relates how surprised he was to have a reunion with two of his actual family ancestors that he had never met in real life.

> *I found myself walking into a barnyard covered with gravel, which I recognized to be the barnyard of a farm that I had often visited when I was a child. It was the barnyard of the farm where my father had grown up. Seated on yard chairs were two elderly men whom I recognized immediately to be my two grandfathers, even though I had never met either of them in my physical life, nor even seen any pictures of them. I started to introduce myself to them, and they both laughed and said—of course, we know who you are. They rose and gave me a high five, much as though I were coming*

out of a basketball game and they had been sitting on the bench. And they both said "Congratulations! A job well done!" And I knew that they meant that I had lived my life in a manner that they approved. I took a seat in a chair next to them and we proceeded to visit about nothing in particular. I had a very warm and satisfying feeling.

In the second account of an ibogaine vision, Wink, who was an avid ocean canoeist, recognized the mystical core and source of his lifelong passion.

I suddenly realized that the ocean is my mother in a manner I do not fully understand. It feels as though if I can allow myself to be embraced by her, that I will be more capable of embracing my family, my friends, my work and myself. Who am I? I am a son of the ocean, the Pacific ocean, the peaceful one, the one who teaches about peace. I am overcome with the feeling that I can feel her breath in the ocean breeze that is blowing up the hill. I am enraptured by her beauty. I feel as though I am gazing at the most beautiful, sensuous woman of all time. She is wife, lover, daughter and granddaughter all wrapped into one. She is absolutely breathtaking! She is massaging me with her waves. She is totally present, so constant with her repetitive motion and at the same time always changing. What a surprise! What is she teaching me, I wondered. To trust in her vastness! To accept the vastness of life!

———

The following two documentaries present footage from the indigenous African iboga cult, as well as discussing its use in the treatment of addiction: *Ibogaine: Rite of Passage,* by Ben de Loenen (2004), and *I'm Dangerous with Love,* by Michael Negroponte (2010).

In the next chapter I will relate a follow-up of sorts to my experiences with ibogaine that occurred in the late 1970s, when I had an opportunity to attend a workshop given in Marin County by the West African healer-teacher Akuete Durchbach.

SEVEN

AKUETE DURCHBACH AND WEST AFRICAN VODOUN

In 1987, about ten years after my initiation experience with iboga, I attended a workshop on spiritual trance healing by a Vodoun ceremonialist and teacher from Togo called Akuete Durchbach. The workshop in San Francisco, sponsored by the Association for Humanistic Psychology (AHP) and the Association for Transpersonal Psychology (ATP), was organized by Danny Slomoff, a graduate student who had made several visits to Togo. He had met and studied with this healer and had written an article about him that was published in the magazine *Shaman's Drum* in 1986. I participated in this workshop with great interest and harbored the intention to ask Akuete Durchbach about iboga, even though I had no reason to believe this plant medicine from the Congo and Zaire was known or used in West Africa.

In the article Danny Slomoff describes meeting Akuete, who was born in 1947 in Togo, finding him to be a "gentle, curious, educated and open man." As a small child he had manifested unusual paranormal events and capabilities, "as though he was possessed by forces and spirits." His family, who were strict Christians, did their best to discourage this direction and sent him to be educated in Paris to study medicine. However, after some years the ancestor spirits started intervening in his life again. "On one occasion there was a knock at his door and the great serpent spirit of Africa entered. He was thrown to the bed and the serpent enveloped him, ending up as a crown on his head. . . . Akuete was no longer able to resist his destiny. He left Europe and returned to Lome (in Togo), changed his life and established himself as a Voodoo priest." The following descriptions of a West African voodoo ceremony are extracted from Slomoff's article in *Shaman's Drum*.

Voodoo is a marvelous, complex religion. Its structure resembles Hinduism, with many spirits and gods. Ceremonies include elements underscoring a sacred relationship to the Earth. The main avenue of spiritual practice is entering a trance state in which one experiences the spirits directly.

A voodoo ceremony in West Africa is a spiritual ritual in which congregants enter an altered state of consciousness through dancing and chanting. The West African priest welcomes the spirits to the ceremony. He prays that they will bless members of the group, enter them and perform wondrous transformations, revelations and healings. The trance is thought of not as a state of availability to the spirits, but as the spirit form entering the human form.

The ritual begins with drumming. While most spirit forms remain unseen in a sacred shrine, one spirit whose form Akuete can reveal is unveiled to the group. It is a three foot statue of an African boy dressed in Western clothes. The ceremony area is prepared with perfumes, water with rose petals and white powder. A member of the congregation walks around the area sprinkling powder and scents. The white powder purifies and attracts spirits. The gods enjoy the sweet smells and are more willing to come to the ceremony. The drumming continues and at a certain moment Akuete joins the group after preparing himself in his sacred shrine.

The songs for the gods and rhythmic drumming and clanging of African bells raises the tempo. A few people break out into dancing, in groups of two, three or four. Men and women walk across the center of the gathering waving their elbows as though they had the wings of fowl. . . . One woman falls to her knees, her body moving in fits, shakes and jerks. She has entered a trance, at one with her gods. Her eyes glass over and an ecstatic smile covers her face.

The congregants are full of caring and concern for one another amid their guests. When people are in trance, the group looks after them, ensuring that they do not hurt themselves, they are comfortable, and their clothes do not fall off, causing embarrassment. I have never witnessed elsewhere the degree of common support and kindness that I experienced among voodooists.

In the state of spirit possession, the community learns important information from the spirits. Perhaps it is a lesson on moral behavior or an important shift in direction the community needs to pursue. Often healings take place. The person in trance might be ill and in need of direct intervention from the spirits.

During the ceremony Akuete performs various tasks. He spends time in his shrine invoking the spirits, praying, making sacrifices of food, fire and alcohol. He also leads the group and urges more intensity and commitment in their prayers so the goods will hear and come. . . . At other times he enters into a trance to contact his higher spiritual guides.

In the workshop I attended, there were not many participants who entered into trance. In fact, perhaps because the audience in the workshop consisted primarily of Euro-Americans from California, Akuete was at pains to emphasize the difference between the kind of controlled, conscious trance cultivated in the West African Vodoun religion and the wild, eye-rolling, screeching trance of popular Hollywood voodoo lore. He said the typical Haitian voodoo as portrayed in such films was a debased form of that religion: they allow or invite the spirits to completely take over the person's will and body. He said in his culture the ceremony leaders keep a close watch on the celebrants. If someone goes into unconscious trance, they take them out of the room, pour cold water over them and bring them back to a normal state of consciousness. He emphasized that the goal is not to allow a spirit to take over your body and oust you, but rather to invite that particular spirit or deity to come into your body. It is like inviting an honored guest into your house for the purposes of a healing ceremony, which you then perform together.

During the workshop, while the participants were in a circle, a pair of drummers were beating out various complex rhythms. Akuete had explained that the drummers know exactly when to shift into the specific rhythms that facilitate entering into trance, and, conversely, when to shift the rhythms again to initiate coming back out of trance to ordinary consciousness, letting the spirits depart. After the rose water and white powder had been sprayed around, Akuete, dressed all in white, moved his feet lightly and in swift rhythmic movements as he danced around the room, making gestures with his hands and arms toward and around the participants standing in a circle. I do not remember the Westerners attending exhibiting trance movements or postures— although the atmosphere was certainly charged with high-frequency energy vibrations. Akuete said that during the ceremonies in his culture, the drummers, who are mostly men, know the particular rhythms that induce the dancers, who are mostly women, to enter into or return from trance.

I came away from the workshop very impressed by Akuete's evident high level of clairvoyant perception and his ability to gently and firmly move people into and out of these healing trances. When preparing this essay almost twenty years after the workshop I had attended with Akuete, I Googled his name and, in addition to Slomoff's 1986 article in *Shaman's Drum,* found the following introductory note written by Mama Zogbé, describing more of the initiatory lineage to which Akuete belonged. This entry also confirmed that Akuete had died in 1996, at the age of forty-seven.

Akuete Durchbach was a master priest of both the Yeveh Vodoun, and the ancient Mami Wata tradition in Togo, West Africa. At the time Danny [Slomoff] wrote this article, very little was known in the West about Mami Wata. As a result, Akuete is referred to as a "Voodoo" priest. Akuete Durchbach was a master shaman who studied for years in the sacred Be (bay) Forest with the aboriginal shamans in Togo. He was crowned Densu, a 300 year old Mami Wata spirit, inherited from his father via his great ancestors. He was Hounon of the Vodoun, being born with all the major Vodoun. He was also a medical doctor, being pulled out of his training by Mami Wata early in his internship. He was respected and feared by many. His power, compassion and knowledge was phenomenal. He helped many people in both Europe and America, as well as in his own village. Masters such as Akuete are rare today even in Africa. I have been blessed to have him physically in my life as both a godparent, teacher and friend for nearly 10 years, and now in spirit as my helper and guide. This article is a rare look into the life of a Master of our ancient African traditions.

———

Since Togo is a francophone culture, Akuete's main European language was French. His translator in the workshops and individual consultations was a large, burly, and cheerful man called Koffi Afawabu. So when I had requested an individual consultation with Akuete, I met with him and Koffi. A few months after the workshop I had attended in mid-1987, I (and presumably others who had attended the workshop) received a letter in which Akuete Durchbach distanced himself and his teachings from Koffi—indicating that "Koffi is not a shaman and might misrepresent himself to you and to capitalize on the momentum that Akuete has initiated in your life. In no way would a workshop with him (Koffi) bring you any closer to Akuete." This was a not uncommon story—spiritual teachers or guides from another culture successfully launch a teaching in the West, and others, unqualified but ambitious, attempt to duplicate their success. I knew nothing of this at the time, and I do not think it detracted from my one private interview with the two men.

I started off by telling Akuete and Koffi that, as a psychologist, I was interested in African shamanic traditions that involve mind-expanding plant substances. I asked whether Akuete could tell me anything about the use of psychoactive herbs in his culture in West Africa, in particular whether they had anything like iboga. His answer was vague and evasive—yes, the traditional shamans in his culture have many plants and herbs that are used for various healing purposes, both physical and mental. I realized that I was being blown off and my attitude was seen as that of a curious but ignorant Westerner, to whom they were not about to reveal cultural secrets. I also sensed that basically they probably did not know about iboga—after all, equatorial Congo and Gabon are several thousand miles and several nation states away from Togo.

I decided to change my approach, and then described in some detail the vision of the African teacher that had appeared to me in my experience with ibogaine, and how he had shown me significant scenes from my childhood. Akuete and his translator listened carefully to my account and then replied—saying, in effect, you have had a genuine experience and received the gift of meeting with a Teacher Spirit. When you have had such a revelation, they emphasized, it is very important that you do not neglect the visionary instructions that you were given, but sincerely dedicate yourself to following their guidance. To do otherwise is to be disrespectful to the spirit that has shown itself to you, and could have negative consequences.

It would be just as disrespectful, with equally negative consequences, they said, if a woman were to reveal her nakedness to you at your request and you then did not make love to her. All three of us seemed to smile or quietly chuckle at that comparison. I thanked the two Africans from Togo for the valuable lesson and took my leave.

EIGHT

LEO ZEFF, ALEXANDER SHULGIN, MDMA, EMPATHY, AND ECSTASY

In the mid-1980s, when MDMA was first created (or rather, re-created as Sasha Shulgin always pointed out), it began to be used as an adjunct to psychotherapy by a handful of therapists on the West Coast, including my esteemed friends and mentors Jack Downing and Leo Zeff. My relationship with them actually went back about twenty years to the mid-1960s, when California was one of the epicenters of a massive sociocultural revolution. Jack Downing had come as a psychiatric observer to the LSD experiments the Leary group conducted in Zihuatanejo, Mexico, in the early 1960s. For a variety of political reasons, that particular project ended in disaster. Ram Dass and I, with Gary Bravo, have described it in our book *Birth of a Psychedelic Culture* (2010). Nevertheless, Downing's published observations on the safety and therapeutic potential of our group sessions with LSD were influential in forming professional opinion.

Joseph "Jack" Downing, M.D. (1924–1993), was chief of medical services in California's San Mateo County. He was also a Gestalt therapist who had studied with Fritz Perls and a Rolfing practitioner who had trained with Ida Rolf. He had participated in the Arica spiritual development program and had been one of the earliest practitioners using LSD therapy for alcoholics. He was my supervising therapist and teacher in the early days of my psychotherapy practice. I always admired him for his openness to new perspectives in spiritually oriented psychotherapy and healing while being grounded in established knowledge and practice.

Leo Zeff (1912–1988) was a psychotherapist who had experimented with some of the substances coming out of Shulgin's laboratory as adjuncts to psychotherapy. Like Jack Downing, he had come to regard MDMA as by far the most promising of these tools. So promising, in fact, that he said he no longer practiced psychotherapy—he just provided the substance and his supportive presence and the clients did all the work themselves.

My introduction to the use of MDMA as an amplifier of psychotherapy came after a ten-year hiatus in my work with psychedelics during the 1970s, when I had focused on learning and practicing the *agni yoga* meditation techniques taught in the School of Actualism. I thought of this period as my time of monastic abstinence from the use of mind-expanding substances in order to focus on step-by-step learning to access and apply the meditation practices.

As fate or fortune would have it, I had also made an earlier connection with Leo Zeff, in the late 1960s or early 1970s, when American culture was in the grip of a prohibitionist drug war that had brought all work with consciousness-expanding substances to a standstill. I was living in Southern California and had written a book called *Maps of Consciousness* (1971), in which I discussed astrology, the *I Ching*, alchemy, tantra, and Actualism—the methods and the system that I was practicing and teaching.

I received an unexpected invitation from Leo Zeff, who as it turned out had known Timothy Leary from the pre-psychedelic days of the 1950s, as colleague psychotherapists in Berkeley. He invited me to come up to a weekend workshop he was conducting somewhere in Northern California and give a guest talk to his group—on selected content from *Maps of Consciousness*. Always the discreet professional, Leo did not really tell me anything about the main focus of the weekend workshop, in which I was to be a guest presenter. Possibly it was my chapter on tantra that was the focus of interest for this group, which turned out to be an experiential practice group for a dozen people from the Morehouse community—about which I knew nothing.

What I have since learned from the internet is that the Morehouse community was founded in 1968 by Victor Baranco in Lafayette in Northern California and still exists, with branches in several cities. The Morehouse philosophy is centered on making sensual pleasure the main practice of your life, with a focus on giving and receiving prolonged full-body orgasms that can last for an hour or more. The practices consist of one person totally receiving and the other person totally focused on "do-ing"—detailed digital manipulation in and around the pelvic organs, releasing full-body orgasmic tremors. So in the workshop arranged by Leo, in which I was a guest presenter, although I was not a participant in the Morehouse practices, I was fascinated to learn, from informal conversations, about such topics as "learning to experience the difference between my anal and vaginal opening."

⎯ ⎯

In mid-1980s, Leo Zeff had basically retired from working as a psychotherapist when, as the legend went, Alexander Shulgin persuaded him to give MDMA a try because of its unique properties of inducing a nonhallucinatory state of balanced empathy, free of anxiety. As I reentered the subculture of therapists using psychedelics in their practices, I was fascinated to learn about MDMA from both Jack Downing and Leo Zeff. In deference to the fast-changing prohibitionist movement, which was making the various mind-assisting drugs illegal almost as fast as Shulgin was creating them, Leo Zeff used the code name *ADAM* for MDMA—which seemed to fit the sense of a primordial beingness that many associated with their experience.

I don't exactly know how Leo Zeff came up with this code name, but I did a little research and found out that the name *Adam* refers to an important symbolic figure in Gnostic texts, about which C. G. Jung wrote extensively. Adam represents "primordial man," "original being," "androgynous ancestor," "man of the Earth," the condition of primal innocence and unity with all life, as described in the biblical account of the Garden of Eden. Feelings of returning to a natural state of innocence, without guilt, shame, or unworthiness, were often reported in experiences with MDMA, as were feelings of connectedness and bonding with fellow human beings, animals, plants, and all the forms and energies of the natural world.

Through my friend the anthropologist Angeles Arrien (1940–2014), I discovered that there was actually a historical group of spiritual seekers called the *Adamites.* Consulting an online encyclopedia, I learned that "this obscure sect, dating probably from the second century [CE], professed to have regained Adam's primeval innocence." They were related to one or more Gnostic sects flourishing during those times. "They called their church *Paradise* claiming that its members were re-established in Adam and Eve's state of original innocence." While some modern people using MDMA or Ecstasy in their rituals would no doubt balk at considering their activities akin to an early Christian liturgy, there are in fact some contemporary groups who take Ecstasy in churchlike gatherings for quiet contemplation—and, of course, others who take it in ecstatic dance raves.

Leo Zeff's pioneering psychotherapy work with MDMA and other substances was first described in a book by Myron Stolaroff called *The Secret Chief.* In the first edition, published in 1997, a pseudonym was given to the psychotherapist whose work was being described. The title of the book was an allusion to a character in Hermann Hesse's short novel *Journey to the East,* published in Germany in 1932. (Tim Leary and I had coauthored an essay in an early issue of the *Psychedelic Review* in which we speculated on apparent psychedelic references in several of Hesse's novels.)

Journey to the East is the story of a group of seekers on a spiritual journey, disguised as a journey to the geographical East. There is a character called Leo, who is a humble and good-humored servant to the pilgrims, and who later turns out actually to be the chief of a secret league of spiritual aspirants. In the Hesse story, Leo never assumed any leading role or title, but "his quiet authority was such that all were happy to follow his guidance." This characterization resonated with people who knew Leo Zeff and the way he worked.

Myron wrote to me in 1998, following the publication of *The Secret Chief,* thanking me for the original source of the concept of "the secret chief."

> I'm also very grateful to learn more about the source of the title, The Secret Chief. When I first heard it, I thought it was a very appropriate title just from what I knew of the family and Jacob's impact on them. I was totally unaware of Hermann Hesse's use of the term. So now he makes profoundly greater sense—an enormous amplification of my previous understanding. And this explanation serves the readers of the book extremely well, giving them a much expanded view of the depth of Jacob's character.

Myron used the title *The Secret Chief* to conceal the identity of the MDMA therapist out of deference to Leo's family's need for privacy and the ability of his collaborator to continue his work. So it was a curious and delightful example of a synchronicity that the reference to the fictional character in Hesse's novel revealed the actual name of the person whose identity was being concealed. The Multidisciplinary Association for Psychedelic Studies (MAPS) finally published the updated edition of his book—*The Secret Chief Revealed: Conversations with Leo Zeff*—in 2005.

Leo Zeff and Jack Downing directly and indirectly introduced and trained a fairly large number of therapists in the use of MDMA for psychotherapy and personal growth, both for individuals and in groups. Shulgin, in an interview (www.mdma.net/alexandershulgin /mdma.html) claimed that Zeff "single-handedly, in the course of about four or five years, distributed it around the world to therapists—not to patients, but to therapists in the thousands. He was probably the Johnny Appleseed of the use of MDMA in psychotherapy." Neither Leo Zeff nor Jack Downing ever wrote up or published their findings—except in a very limited way, preferring to carry on their work of coaching other therapists beneath the prohibitionist radar.

Both Leo Zeff and Jack Downing contributed pseudonymous case reports from their files to the anthology of experiences with MDMA that a small group of us compiled and self-published in 1985 called *Through the Gateway of the Heart*—and both of them also contributed financially to its publication. For our protection, I used the pseudonym "Sophia Adamson" (with allusions to the wisdom goddess, the substance ADAM, and the Adamites) as the listed author, because the book came out in 1985, the same year MDMA was put on Schedule I (for drugs with high potential for abuse and, supposedly, no known medical use). It was out of print for some twenty years, but was republished in a new edition with updated introductory and supporting material by Padma Catell and me in 2012.

Fig. 8.1. Cover image of *Through the Gateway of the Heart*. Cover art by Susan Seddon Boulet

Before coming into contact with Leo, I had never really experienced or conducted individual psychotherapy with psychedelics. My model for guidance was the one described in *The Psychedelic Experience,* based on *The Tibetan Book of the Dead.* By the time I met him in the mid-1980s, I was moving toward the collaboratively self-directed trip. It was Leo Zeff who introduced me to the use of MDMA and I was deeply impressed and touched by the empathic, nondirective yet supportive way he conducted the sessions. Although he was a Jungian trained and experienced psychotherapist, by this time in his career and with this new medicine, he said he just "tripped" people and let them do all their healing work themselves. He was supportively present and would answer questions when asked, but otherwise let people work on their own self-identified issues, while listening to self-selected music. His work with entheogens had a psychospiritual orientation, and he would offer meditative prayer-like readings from books such as *A Course in Miracles* in the preparatory phase of sessions that he guided.

I resonated deeply with his approach to guiding—both compassionate and friendly, serious and yet with a light touch. I remember how touched I was during my introductory session with MDMA, when he gave me a glass of water to drink, with a bent straw that enabled me

Fig. 8.2. Leo Zeff in 1987. Photo by Ralph Metzner

Fig. 8.3. Leo Zeff (right) and Terence McKenna, in Hawaii, 1987.
Photo by Ralph Metzner

to drink in a semi-reclining position without sitting up. He would sit nearby in the same room where I was reclining with eye-shades on to focus inner awareness. He told me he would be reading a light, entertaining book, nothing serious, so that he would be immediately available in case I had any questions that came up.

Leo's nondirective, yet caring and receptive approach to conducting sessions with MDMA seemed to resonate perfectly with the kind of experience this medicine offered. It was not a "nonordinary" or hallucinatory state of consciousness, with potentials for surprising and frightening visions. It just seemed to open one to the ordinary reality and acceptance of one's state of being in a totally positive way. From my conversations with Leo, I surmised that he had decided that the most effective contribution he could make to the spread of this perfectly legal, as yet unknown drug was to supply it to psychotherapists who were interested and coach them in its best use.

Over the next few years, while MDMA was still legal, Leo and I met occasionally so that I could renew my supplies and consult with him about difficult issues that had come up in therapy sessions. I heard him complain a couple of times that the drug had such a positive effect that he had to intervene with some therapists he had trained that were using it too frequently, addictively, or in a way that mixed up the roles of therapist and patient. The erosion of professional boundaries that can occur with the noncareful use of MDMA in psychotherapy was one of the factors contributing to its popularization and subsequent prohibition.

A few years ago, a friendly little debate arose in the pages of the *MAPS Bulletin* about whether MDMA should be called *entactogenic* ("inducing an inner touching"), a term proposed by chemist David Nichols, or *empathogenic* ("inducing an empathic response"), which was the term I proposed. Readers weighed in on one side or the other, and no consensus emerged. I argued that "touching within" doesn't really distinguish MDMA-type drugs from other psychedelics, all of which touch the inner realms of consciousness. A facilitation of empathy, for others and for self, seemed to me to be the key to its usefulness in psychotherapy. On the other hand, I recognize that the drug per se doesn't induce empathy—unless that is the intention or predisposition of the individual in the context of the situation. The thousands of ravers who take Ecstasy to dance the night away aren't necessarily having an empathic experience, or an inner spiritual experience, for that matter. That said, it does appear that more of the European researchers use the term *entactogen,* whereas more of the American researchers use *empathogen.*

Impeccable scientist that he was, Alexander "Sasha" Shulgin (1925–2014) understood immediately after his first self-experiment with mescaline in the late 1950s that the drug was not the cause of his experience; rather, it released something that "came from the depths of my memory and my psyche." He incorporated that understanding into three decades of research, which resulted in his two astonishing and monumental contributions to the scientific study of consciousness, coauthored with his wife and partner, Ann Shulgin: *PIHKAL (Phenethylamines I Have Known and Loved)* and *TIHKAL (Tryptamines I Have Known and Loved)*. Both books are organized in two parts, autobiographical and chemical. The first four hundred pages of *PIHKAL* narrate Sasha's and Ann's meeting and their relationship as it evolved into a marriage and working partnership. The next five hundred pages contain Shulgin's detailed description of the chemistry and synthesis of 179 phenethylamines, with their effects on consciousness, described from self-experiments. *TIHKAL* is similar: four hundred pages of conjoint autobiography, followed by descriptions of the synthesis of psychoactive tryptamines. The book is rounded out by encyclopedic information about the chemistry of cactus alkaloids, carbolines, and histamines, as well as commentaries on drug legislation and politics.

Surely there has never been such a work, "a sort of sorcerer's book of spells," as David Nichols says in his foreword to *PIHKAL*. They

Fig. 8.4. Alexander Shulgin in his lab, 1995. Photo by Ralph Metzner

Fig. 8.5. Alexander Shulgin, demonstrating molecular structures with his hands at a lecture, 1998. Photo by Ralph Metzner

are detailed how-to manuals of mostly prohibited psychoactive chemicals, written in the internationally recognized language of chemistry, so that in some other country or time, scientists will be able to make these fascinating tools, many of which Shulgin was the first to discover or create. No one who has ever seen and heard him speak can forget the passion, the flashing eyes, and vivid gestures with which he conjured molecular structures in the air, explaining how they fit together. And there has surely never been such an unusual combination work of organic chemistry synthesis, qualitative assessment of subjective effects in the human psyche, and personal autobiography of the scientist and his spouse and collaborator. Their work harks back to an age before the so-called "scientific revolution" in the sixteenth century, when alchemy and chemistry were still united as one science integrating observation and experiment with both *physis* and *psyche*.

Recognizing that animal studies of mind-altering pharmaceuticals provide very little useful information about their action in humans, Shulgin opted instead for the time-honored method of self-experimentation. In the introduction to *PIHKAL*, he wrote, "Psychedelic drugs provide access to the parts of us which have answers. They can, but again, they need not and probably will not, unless that is the purpose for which they are being used." He forcefully states the case against doing so-called double-blind studies: in the case of psychoactive drugs, where the main effects can only be observed in one's own sensorium and psyche, their use "verges upon the unethical." As unethical, one might say, as sending someone on an exploration of a foreign land without having been there oneself. As natural philosophers from Heraclitus to the alchemists have said, there is no other way to study the working of the mind than in one's own mind, in collaboration with others.

In his two autobiographies, Shulgin describes how he created each drug in his laboratory, following his molecular intuition in a way that only a highly trained and gifted chemist could. He then tested each new drug with a constant group of collaborators that included himself,

Fig. 8.6. Alexander and Ann Shulgin, at a retreat conference in Palenque, Mexico, 1999. Photo by Ralph Metzner

his wife Ann, and a dozen research associates. This group met together and sampled each new compound that he created in his laboratory. He established a safe dosage range and developed a five-point scale of subjective intensity on which he and his associates rated each compound. Considering the effects of psychedelic compounds to be a function of three factors—substance, dosage, and set-and-setting—he set up a research protocol that held the set and setting factors constant, which allowed for meaningful comparisons between different substances at different dosage levels. The constant setting for these studies was a comfortable home, and the consistent set or intention was to make comparative observations of each new substance that the chemist had created.

Certain rules of etiquette were agreed to by all, and precautions and procedural signals were established so that participants could veto any aspect of the situation with which they were uncomfortable. Very importantly also, rules relating to sexual activity during each experiment were formalized; these essentially allowed private sexual expression for couples in another part of the house, while otherwise respecting appropriate boundaries in the shared space of the meeting.

It would be hard to overstate the significance of Shulgin's scientific contribution described in these two volumes. While Erowid, the ongoing internet-based encyclopedia of psychoactive drug experiences, does provide useful preliminary observations on different drugs, we have to consider that the set and setting factors for each set of observations can vary enormously and confound the differences between substances. Scientifically, Sasha's reports provide much more useful information. In his reporting, the set and setting variables are held constant, and the reports are from a consistent group of seasoned observers. So we can be reasonably certain that differences observed between the experiences of the different compounds are in fact due to the particular actions of that compound in the human observer.

Though Sasha Shulgin created MDMA and other drugs and described their chemical structure in the professional scientific journals he was always scrupulously careful to avoid any involvement in the diversion of these drugs into the wider marketplace of drug users. He did supply MDMA to Leo Zeff, who distributed it to his network of psychotherapists, including myself, while it was still legal, but otherwise Shulgin's human studies were solely within his small research group. He was exclusively concerned with contributing to the body of published scientific knowledge. His scientific papers detailing the synthesis of these drugs were published in the chemistry journals and could be read by anyone who understood that scientific language. But he did not want to be associated in any way with producing drugs for the underground recreational market. Sometimes he worked with law-enforcement officials, helping them identify drugs that had been seized and were as yet unknown.

At one point in the mideighties, I unexpectedly found myself in the crosshairs of Sasha's disapproval. A man from Texas named Michael Clegg came into one of my groups in which we used MDMA in a circle format, alternating periods of quiet introspection with periods of speaking empathically and from the heart. I never supplied the drug, though it was still legal, to people for their own use. But Clegg was enthusiastic about the substance and wanted to produce and distribute it himself. He found a chemist to make it using Shulgin's own published papers. Then he brought it to me and asked if I would ask Shulgin to examine it for quality and purity. I knew that Sasha often analyzed drugs produced in the underground, so I asked him. He did and reported back to me that it was indeed high-quality MDMA. I reported this back to Michael Clegg and thereby inadvertently crossed Sasha's prohibition line. He did not want underground drug makers and dealers to be saying, "This was tested and certified by Shulgin."

As Sasha said in an interview (www.mdma.net), "Outside of therapeutic community there was, as there almost always is in these cases, a person or a few people who figured out they could sell MDMA and make a lot of money. They were the ones who gave it the name 'ecstasy.' The drug should have been called 'empathy' for what it did, but I believe they felt that empathy didn't have the same sensational ring to it. So they called it *Ecstasy,* which is a strange name but it stuck. And it was sold more and more at bars, parties, what have you. The whole thing came to a crisis in Texas where it was used to such an extent that the authorities became concerned and decided that since it was a recognized drug that came under the umbrella of a pharmaceutical house, it was therefore an abusable drug which needed to be made illegal."

From a sociological point of view, this MDMA story in the 1980s was more or less a replay of what happened with LSD and other psychedelics in the 1960s: A promising new drug is discovered or invented as an adjunct for psychotherapy with wide-ranging applications. The drug has minimal physical effects but has huge potentials for healing, psychotherapy, creativity, expanding consciousness, and spiritual growth—far beyond the classic psychiatric paradigms. Enterprising independent chemists figure out the manufacturing process from published literature, and distribution networks arise. The medical and governmental bureaucracies react with shock and propaganda campaigns to demonize the drug and instill fear in the population (fear of *what* exactly, one might ask?). Sanctioned research at academic institutions comes to a standstill. The drug goes underground as a recreational substance and is used for dance parties—acid tests in the 1960s, raves in the 1980s. The enormous positive potentials remain relatively unexplored.

⸺

Like other therapists in the early 1980s, using this as yet unknown and unprohibited catalyst, I quickly recognized while the set-and-setting hypothesis applied to MDMA also, this substance nevertheless had certain unique properties compared to the classic psychedelics like LSD or mescaline. With MDMA, individuals were able, if their intention in taking the substance was serious and therapeutic, to use the state to resolve, more or less by themselves, long-standing intrapsychic conflicts and/or problems in interpersonal relationships. One therapist acquaintance of mine estimated that in five hours of one MDMA session, clients could activate and process psychic material that would normally require five months of weekly therapy sessions.

In fact, I believe that MDMA spread underground, outside of therapists' auspices, partly because many people perceived that they could use it to do most of their healing work on relationships themselves, without the aid (and expense) of a therapist—if the substance was available to them. As one of the therapists in that first wave associated with Leo Zeff, I found more than once that clients, working their way through interpersonal communication issues in a single MDMA session, made some decisions about changes needed in their relationships, said "thank you," and never came back. Such observations threw an unexpected monkey wrench into the usual assumption that interpersonal issues require months or years of psychotherapy and working through a transference relationship with the therapist. I am one of many people I know who have no particular interest in taking MDMA again, because I can access the feeling state of empathic equanimity simply by recalling it. The only occasion I would want to take it myself would be to work on some relationship issue with my partner.

The fact that this substance enabled people to do self-directed relationship healing contributed, I believe, to its rapid spread in underground circles. In a classic example of the American entrepreneurial spirit—"identify a need and meet it"—people figured out the chemistry, usually from Shulgin's books, and arranged to supply their own MDMA. Of course, once that process got started, there was no longer any way to restrict the availability of a perfectly legal drug only to therapists. Pretty soon *Ecstasy* was being sold in bars and on college campuses in Texas and was being distributed at raves. Inevitably as night follows day, the drug was made illegal, and distribution networks went underground. Production was unregulated, so quality control became hit-or-miss. Therapists like me, who had used MDMA with excellent results, could no longer obtain it for their work with clients.

A certain commonality existed in the kinds of feeling states that people reported regarding their initial experiences with MDMA, using words such as *empathy, openness, compassion, peace, acceptance, forgiveness, healing, oneness,* and *caring.* There weren't any reports of hallucinatory "bummers" or torturous "bad trips," as there were with the classical psychedelics. In fact, there weren't any visions or hallucinations at all. People just reported hitherto unknown levels of positive and affirmative feeling—toward themselves and toward others. As an example, in her first experience with MDMA, one woman observed a kind of knot in her heart center. As she focused warmth and caring attention on it, it seemed to literally loosen and unravel; simultaneously, she was aware that several of her personal relationships were somehow being healed. At the end, she felt much more positive about each of these relationships. Another client of mine, who had experienced LSD and a variety of other psychedelics, said on his first experience with MDMA, "Everything looks just the same, but I *feel* completely different about it."

Various forms of bodywork and massage can also be amplified in their range and depth if the recipient's awareness has been sensitized by MDMA at lower dosages. The usual report from such experiences is that the recipient of the bodywork who has taken MDMA is in an ultra-relaxed state in which every bodily movement and response is experienced with less resistance and a much greater range. The effects of finger pressure on the shoulder, for example, might be felt in a connected flow of sensory awareness all the way to the feet.

It goes perhaps without saying (but nevertheless is still worth saying) that in all individual and group therapeutic sessions with MDMA and similar empathogens, the ethical guidelines for the behavior of clients and therapists must be explicitly discussed and agreed upon prior to the session. We have seen how in Sasha Shulgin's groups, which are scientific-exploratory and not therapy-oriented, there were nevertheless explicit ethical codes of interpersonal behavior, especially in the sexual arena. It is equally important to adhere to the commonly accepted ethical guidelines in individual therapy or bodywork when amplified by MDMA/Ecstasy.

Through the Gateway of the Heart provides several accounts that highlight the unusually clear differentiation between sexuality and sensuality that is characteristic of the Adamic ecstasy experience associated with MDMA. People often report feeling emotionally intimate, and being able to easily share deep feelings in a kind of emotional mergence with others, but not particularly sexually aroused or even interested. This quality of the experience may be the reason why people can attend Ecstasy raves with thousands of others, dancing with abandon and sharing intimate conversations without feeling threatened by unwanted approaches or even interested in any longer-term connection.

In some Esalen gatherings that took place in the early 1980s, I decided to test this Adamic perception of nonsexual intimacy by having two sessions with an Esalen masseuse on separate days—one in which I took MDMA and one in which I didn't. I wrote up this delightful experiment pseudonymously in *Through the Gateway of the Heart*. The "control" experience, by the attractive nude masseuse, was pleasurable, with the usual accompaniment of desire-fuelled fantasies. The experience of massage by the same masseuse, after I had taken 50 milligrams of MDMA, I described as *tantric:* "Desire was transcended by being fulfilled as there was nothing else that I wanted."

In this and other accounts, people report feeling emotionally merged with the other and desirous of close physical contact, perhaps holding hands, but without striving for heightened sensation or orgasmic release. There is typically no desire for further merging or penetration and also little or no tumescence in the genitalia. Subjectively, it's as if complete sensual and emotional bonding is already taking place, so genital conjunction seems redundant.

An unexpected confirmation of this kind of "genital-bypass" effect of MDMA was related to me by a former psychotherapy client who had gone to Peru to participate in ayahuasca ceremonies with a well-known shaman. This particular shaman was known for having sex with Western women who participated in his ceremonies—always claiming, of course, that each one was "special." When the woman gave him a dose of this new Western medicine to try, he despised it, because the lack of tumescence in his sexual organ inhibited his shamanic powers, as he claimed.

It has seemed to me for a long time that the nonsexual emotional intimacy facilitated by MDMA is a reason both for its astonishing efficacy in psychotherapy—where sexual feelings toward the therapist are regarded as an inappropriate "transference"—and the reason for its amazing safety record in rave dance parties involving hundreds of participants. When I became aware of the research with MDMA carried out by Dr. Torsten Passie, a German psychiatrist working at the University of Hanover who has reported on individual and group psychotherapy with MDMA and also studied the neurophysiological and neuropharmacological correlates of the experience, I realized that he has identified what is perhaps the essential and unique element in this remarkable medicine.

On the basis of his studies, Passie states that MDMA deactivates the amygdala (the seat of fear-rage emotional reactivity) and reciprocally activates prefrontal brain circuits (which underlie calm thinking). This is the neurophysiological counterpart to the empathic understanding of self and others that is reported by the patients. There is also a massive release of serotonin, the neurotransmitter associated with a nondepressive, nonfearful attitude.

To my mind, the most interesting and suggestive of Passie's findings is that MDMA results in a release of prolactin, the hormone associated with breast-feeding, which is also released naturally during nonsexual postorgasmic intimacy.

Several studies have demonstrated a marked increase of prolactin plasma levels after MDMA/MDEA consumption together with an impairment of sexual drive and function in humans. Clinical and experimental evidence suggest a possible role for prolactin in mediating a state of relaxation and sexual refractoriness after both orgasm and during the acute effects of MDMA/MDEA. (Passie, et al., 2005)

As Passie points out, the release of nonsexual intimacy hormones correlates perfectly with the often-remarked subjective experience of MDMA users: they feel intimate with others, wanting to touch and be physically close, but are not sexually aroused at all. Even couples who are intimately involved have reported that with MDMA, the sexual drive is often just not there. Several women who have had children have also confirmed that, at its best, the MDMA experience is comparable to the blissful feelings of merging and fusion experienced by mother and infant during lactation.

If prolactin release is the hormonal basis (or at least one of the factors responsible) for the outpouring of empathic and telepathic communion characteristic of the MDMA experience, it is not surprising that it counteracts fear, trauma, distrust, separation anxiety, and the like. MDMA stimulates the hormones of nursing and postorgasmic bliss—archetypal opposites of fear and isolation/separation.

In the mid-1980s, when the unique qualities of the MDMA experience were first becoming recognized, a group of scientists and psychotherapists were convened at Esalen by Stan and Christina Grof to discuss and explore the implications and possibilities of Shulgin's remarkable discovery. Albert Hofmann, then already in his eighties, attended this meeting and expressed his appreciation for the unitive experience this substance could produce. "With this substance, matter and mind are one," as he put it in one of our group sessions at that time.

Teachers and practitioners of meditation and other forms of spiritual work have described the MDMA experience as being fundamentally an opening of the heart center. This center (called the *anahata chakra* in the Indian yoga system), considered to be related to healing, is involved in all interpersonal relationships; it also amplifies the feeling connection to the higher realms of Spirit. One meditation teacher suggested that the MDMA experience helps dissolve the barriers between body, mind, and spirit.

At one point in the early 1990s, after MDMA had escaped from the relatively small circle of California therapists into the mainstream culture, becoming the simultaneously popular and illegal drug known as Ecstasy, virtually all the residents of the Rajneesh ashram in Oregon were said to be using it regularly as a support for their meditation practice. Of course, the subsequent history of the Rajneesh ashram, with its tales of physical abuse, financial corruption, and flagrant criminality demonstrates (again) that temporarily enhanced positive and even spiritual feeling states do not necessarily lead to enhanced responsible behavior.

In the typical Adamic ecstasy experience with MDMA, mind and body can be effortlessly coordinated: an empathic positive attitude, so significant for interpersonal relationships, also becomes the attitude toward one's own body, which in turn feels accepted and protected. Thus instinctual awareness, as well as mental, emotional, and sensory awareness, can all function together, rather than one being the focus at the expense of the others. Similarly, Spirit or Higher Self is no longer felt as a remote, abstract concept, "above" somewhere; rather one senses the presence of Spirit infusing the structures of the body and the images and attitudes of the mind. Awareness is expanded to include all parts of the body, all aspects of the mind, and the higher spiritual realms of consciousness. This permits a kind of reconnecting, a remembering of the totality of experience, an access to forgotten truth.

Reading accounts like those in *Through the Gateway of the Heart,* one is struck by how people often express their realizations in the form of seemingly banal statements—such as that one only needs love and all else falls into place, or that coming from the heart all other choices are easy and right. But the statements are *felt* with an intensity that belies their seeming banality. These observations and experiences suggest that the greatest potential of this substance may lie in the self-training of psychotherapists. The ability to experience and articulate empathy toward the patient is often regarded as the most important criterion of effective psychotherapy. Psychotherapists who have experienced MDMA affirm that besides their own personal learning, they also frequently have insights into their clients' problems.

The predictably positive response to empathogens makes them an ideal treatment support for traumatized individuals. The last thing you want in psychotherapy for PTSD is for the traumatic experience to be replayed in excruciating detail, with all the pain and shock of the original. Instead the individual needs to be able to recall and relate the trauma with an assured underlying attitude of empathy for self and others. A study by Gillinder Bedi et al. (2009) used functional magnetic-resonance imaging in healthy volunteers viewing images depicting different emotional facial expressions under two different doses of MDMA. The authors concluded that MDMA attenuated amygdala response to angry facial expressions, did not affect brain responses to fearful stimuli, and enhanced brain responsiveness to faces expressing happy emotions. A related study by Bedi et al. (2010) suggested that the increased empathic response to MDMA was seemingly accompanied by inaccurate perception of threatening facial expressions—a kind of "see no evil" attitude.

A consensus appears to be emerging that it is in the treatment of PTSD that MDMA-facilitated therapy will find its first approved place in mainstream medicine and psychiatry. This is especially true considering the huge numbers of traumatized soldiers and veterans from America's global wars that are treated only superficially, with tranquilizers and sedatives. Their appallingly high suicide rate shows the total inadequacy of current approaches. Getting FDA/DEA final approval for MDMA therapy may take five or more years and could cost $50 million—but compared to the cost of medical and rehabilitative care in this population, this is small change. Initial research studies by Michael and Annie Mithoefer using MDMA to treat both sexual trauma and war trauma, along with other projects sponsored by the MAPS organization, are enormously promising.

When I was collecting the stories published in *Through the Gateway of the Heart,* two different psychotherapists that were starting to use MDMA, one of them being Jack Downing, sent in case studies of rape and violence victims who were almost completely healed after a small number of MDMA-therapy sessions. When the Senate subcommittee was holding hearings in 1985 about how MDMA should be scheduled, Jack appeared with one of his clients, who testified that her therapy sessions with MDMA had enabled her to recover the dissociated memory of a horrific rape assault. She said that the healing process had begun, but she felt she needed more sessions with MDMA to complete the healing. Despite her testimony and the recommendations of the subcommittee, the Senate ultimately voted to put MDMA in the most restrictive category, Schedule I—of "drugs with no recognized healing value," where it has been ever since, along with heroin, cocaine, amphetamine, LSD, and others.

Through the Gateway of the Heart also contained an account I wrote with Ed Ellis. It is the story of a Vietnam veteran from the early years of the war, who, in the course of a single MDMA-therapy session, was able to identify and release an enormous pressure cooker of suppressed fear from the war situation and transform that energy into peace activism. I will discuss this study, along with the subsequent individual and social healing work done by Ed Ellis, in the next chapter.

In the late 1980s, I was asked to work with an activist from South America who had been imprisoned by the military junta and brutally tortured over a period of several days. I was following the process guidelines developed by the outstanding pioneer of trauma therapy Peter Levine, Ph.D. (who does not use MDMA). In this process, the recalling and relating of the traumatic experience is "calibrated" in small segments, interspersed with returns to the established place of confirmed safety in present time. I first asked the man to empathically connect with a totally calm and safe emotional attitude, while relating the general circumstances of his arrest and imprisonment. This was then the psychic space of safety, amplified by MDMA, from which he related, in small segments, the tortures that he had endured, and screamed his pain (muffled with a cloth stuffed into his mouth), going back to the safe space after each segment.

Psychotherapy with victims of torture is known for posing special countertransference issues for the therapist, who might have difficulty maintaining a stance of empathic neutrality. When working with this client, I struggled with vengeful rage at the appalling behavior of his tormenters. But in his empathic state, the client himself was not diverted into any trace of punitive reaction. In this gradually calibrated process, the MDMA amplified the basic self-empathic posture at the basis of healing. For obvious reasons, this form of therapy could not be used in cases where the victim was forcibly given different kinds of drugs—but apart from that, MDMA therapy offers great hope in these kinds of horrendous situations.

———

In yet another paradoxical wrinkle, even while we can acknowledge the primacy of set and setting over the specific drug in accounting for most of the content of a therapeutic MDMA experience, on some occasions the substance itself seems to overrule these factors. The following beautiful "miracle" story was related to me by my long-term friend George Douvris, who gave me permission to publish it in my blog. Since then, he has also related it in his autobiography (Douvris, 2016, 353–4). George, who had himself experienced some deep healing with MDMA, was visiting his aging mother in Greece, along with his wife Stephanie and their three teenage children.

> The setting was a traditional home in a Greek village. This was the house my mother had grown up in before emigrating to the United States as a young lady. The room she stayed in was exactly like she had left it seventy five years previously, with the same bed and wall decorations. We had brought her back to this house when she was around 94 and were taking care of her as needed.

She was fairly well until the last year when her health deteriorated rapidly. No longer could she walk without trembling, nor do much in the way of independent action and thought. She was 99 years old and had made it clear that she wanted to die here in her home and be buried with her ancestors. Yet her anger at us and the world in general continued to consume her passion.

It was on such an evening of her cursing my existence that I reflected deeply on her situation. Under normal circumstances I would consider it unethical to give someone a drug without explaining to them the purpose and its possible side-effects. But in this situation of her being caught in such a web of emotional pain and negativity, I decided to give the one dose of MDMA which I was saving for a special occasion.

As she grabbed the little white pill that I gave her, my mother hissed the question "what are you giving me?" to which I replied that it was "heart medicine." Her retort was that I had been giving her poison to her heart all my life and here was one more intention of mine to kill her. I took a deep breath and felt a fearful premonition that her experience could be a very, very bad one. It would then be a decision that would haunt me for the rest of my life. It turned out to be true that the decision had a significant impact on my life but with a far better outcome than I anticipated. After giving her the "heart medicine" I said my good nights and left her alone.

Checking in half an hour later, I found her sitting on her bed gazing at an icon of the Virgin Mary. Her smiling was a hint that a profound event was manifesting. When I asked her how she felt, she said softly that there were "angels flying around the room." I ran upstairs and woke up our son John, telling him to come downstairs with his guitar—that we had important work to do with his grandmother.

For the next few hours we exchanged hugs with my mother and shared her delight in listening to CDs of Greek Orthodox religious hymns as well as her favorite Greek folk music. When Stephanie came downstairs to be part of the miracle, she asked my mother how she was doing—to which my mom said in a very sweet tone "this night will never end." Her words, smiles and touch were soft and loving. It was a blessing for all of us.

There was more amazement ahead. From that night on, for the last seven months of her life, my mother dropped her fear-based masking and let her heart express itself in a very beautiful way. No longer would she judge or criticize anyone but instead made only loving remarks. She would smile and ask to kiss us regularly every day. She no longer demanded that I cut my beard but asked if she could stroke it. She had previously refused to let her granddaughters take her to the village in her wheelchair. Now she welcomed their brushing her hair, putting a flower in back of her ear and taking her out for ice cream.

The experience with the "heart-medicine" brought lasting comfort in her remaining life and could well have helped her soul cross over more gently. The circle was complete and her grandchildren will always remember her as being at peace with herself and the world.

When George told me this story, he and I both realized that his mother had been totally released from what seemed in retrospect like a malignant curse. We also both recognized that he had violated the implicit and explicit code of ethics observed by all psychedelic explorers—not to give a psychedelic drug to someone without their knowledge and consent—and had taken a chance in so doing. But he also realized that there was no way that he could explain what the medicine was or predict what the effects would be. The deep soul connection and trust between mother and son, and their basic integrity, outweighed the more superficial, fearful, and paranoid ideation that afflicted the old lady.

NINE

FROM TRAUMATIZED VETERAN
TO PEACEMAKER ACTIVIST

In the mid-1980s I was contacted by Ed Ellis, a veteran of the Vietnam War who was dealing with residual trauma of his time in the war more than ten years previously. He wrote me saying he had experimented with LSD a little before going to Vietnam and had several profound experiences with it while there, but also several "bummers." He wrote, "I had these incredible euphoric trips where I felt I loved everyone and was at complete peace with myself." But then he went on a bummer he couldn't be talked out of, and he felt abandoned by the friend who had been his trip companion. He suffered a nervous breakdown and was "fucked up," as he put it. He wrote in a letter, "What I can't get out of my head is: I'm still off from my last LSD experience. I still feel somewhat unclear and slightly depressed. I miss the feeling of complete well-being and connection to everyone and everything I had during my LSD trips—when my mind went out to the ends of the universe and I felt so connected to everything. I could feel a bird flying by me. The most profound feeling I ever had." After the bummers, he said he felt like a sailor without a ship. He believed he couldn't get clear without taking acid again, but was afraid.

When my tour in Vietnam ended in 1970, I returned to my home town in northern Oregon. This was a difficult period of suffering, introspection and hedonism. I was bothered by guilt from serving in Vietnam, and an incomplete feeling from several bad acid trips, as well as panic attacks. My enemy was an unease that subtracted from social interactions. An army buddy and I moved to Hawaii and drove taxi, living an irresponsible life, heavily seasoned with sex, drugs and free-floating anxieties.

After about three years Ed moved to Los Angeles and entered a residential therapy program at the Primal Institute. "Primal therapy helped me to get rid of what I didn't need and come to an understanding of my own history. The tears evoked during the therapy humanized me and I opened more to my wife, children and my work as a gardener. The years passed, as did my parents, and during this time I would often remember the profound acid trips I had in Vietnam and how they had opened up new levels of consciousness. These states of cosmic consciousness would stay with me for several weeks and I'd feel as if I had crossed the threshold of Heaven. But I also carried an uneasy feeling, a kind of dread associated with my Vietnam tour."

When I asked Ed to describe his experience of being in the Vietnam War, he said he had not been physically wounded, but their base could be and was often attacked, at any time of the day or night, so there was a constant high level of fear. This struck me as the worst possible set and setting for a productive psychedelic experience. When I asked him why he took LSD there at all, with that ever-present threat, he replied that he and his buddies all knew that they could be killed at any time—so why not take the chance and have this experience while you still could? He described being high on acid at night, standing in the pouring rain with his arms ecstatically stretched out to the heavens. If there was a sudden attack, they would have to come down and get ready—and they did.

Many years after this conversation with Ed Ellis, I learned from my friend Nick Sand (1941–2017), the renowned LSD chemist who served time in jail for his pharmaceutical activities, that he had supplied thousands of gratis doses of LSD to U.S. army soldiers during the Vietnam War and may have been the supplier for Ed's enlightenment experiences. Synchronicity again!

Ed had gone to Vietnam an idealistic young patriot, expecting to help his country defeat communism. Within a short time, he and most of his buddies realized the whole mission was a sham—they were invading and occupying another country. After that, their main preoccupation became how to get out of there alive. "I was carrying a lot of fear and a lot of blame. Blame towards my government for bringing horror to the people of Vietnam and blame toward myself for participating in it."

A short while after we started our therapeutic talking sessions, we both realized that further probing of the bad acid trips in Vietnam was pointless. I pointed out that being in that dangerous war setting was a guaranteed bad trip; the greater paradox was the occurrence of his ecstatic trips. And his real concern, after all, was with the lingering depression and anxiety—now ten years after his deployment. At that time I was one of about a dozen or so therapists, many in California, who had started using MDMA as an adjunct and amplifier for psychotherapy. I suggested working with this medicine to heal the trauma rather than using LSD to probe deeper meanings of the trauma. Ed readily agreed.

During his first MDMA session, I began by asking him to describe his mental and emotional state while he was there on his tour of duty. He said it was one of constant terror due to the possibility of being attacked unexpectedly, at any time of the day or night. He started to weep. He had felt almost as if he were not entitled to feel or express fear. Nothing physically traumatic had happened to him—and anyway the soldier's ethic was just to "suck it up." For the first time since returning from his tour of duty, he could acknowledge the abject terror of just being in that place and time of war—and could weep real tears for the terrified young man he was.

In a letter to me written after the MDMA session, Ed wrote, "That session with you was a turning point for me. I have been aware of a deep sadness ever since and have been having a lot of emotional release. These tears have been such a friend to me. I have periods of deep sadness and it frees me up, as I stand in the middle of my life and look around with such thankfulness to be here—to be alive and to sense the processes of my life. I had been afraid to see any of the films about the war and afraid to talk to anyone, even my wife, about the fear and grief around the war experience. Then I decided to see *Platoon* and was so shocked I could barely talk." He told me he actually went to see Oliver Stone's film several times, sometimes with one of his buddies, as well as with his wife. It was as if floodgates of terror, grief, and shame had been opened, and for the first time he found he could talk about being in the war. He wrote, "I was achieving more awareness of what happened to me—and to this country. I don't think this country is over what it did in Vietnam at all."

From that session, he and I both realized that the real trauma for him was not the bad acid trips he had in Vietnam, but just the fact of being there, in that war with which he was in total moral disagreement. He hadn't been physically wounded, so the moral conflict had been covered over in his mind. Furthermore, as a soldier, he thought he somehow didn't have a right to feelings of terror and grief. It became clear to me, from this experience and others, that MDMA was much better suited for healing the painful terror-trauma and associated denial than probing with LSD would have been.

In another one of his letters, Ed wrote:

The process of opening to these feelings was accelerated by the Gulf War of 1991, which broke open what I had been carrying around and directed me toward more therapy and rap sessions with other vets. It also motivated me to join the group Veterans for Peace *in Los Angeles and become a peacemaker. In 1994 I became president and organized a veterans speakers group with twelve other vets. We visited high school classrooms throughout Los Angeles, shared our war stories and encouraged the students to think of nonviolent solutions to conflict. We talked of the war propaganda in the media and the brainwashing going on of our own American history, the whitewashing of many dark events. We knew this wasn't about war stories, but the honest telling of painful experiences with tears of grief.*

The students were receptive as were the teachers, because the truths we spoke relaxed our guts and we finally felt that things made sense. We encouraged each other to also speak what had not been said publically to friends and to family. We were asked back year after year. Our talks were particularly powerful in the schools of East Los Angeles, like Garfield and Manual Arts, where college recruiters are not seen and military recruiters are seen constantly. In some schools we saw recruiters teaching gym class and being a permanent fixture in the lunch room. We realized what a scam the recruiters were pulling—promising a college education if the students would risk their lives. We debated the recruiters and in one session the recruiter was so ill-informed that she elicited critical responses from the students. She later broke down in tears, telling us that she didn't want to be doing this—basically processing fresh meat for the American war machine. The teachers also were supportive—they would invite us into the classrooms directly, bypassing the paperwork. This was a powerful learning experience for me and I got a lot of help from the teachers with speaking.

The speaking events in high schools went on, and at the beginning of the Iraq war in 2003, Ed and his fellow Veterans for Peace began including younger Gulf War veterans in their talks with the students. To develop a new strategy, the Los Angeles Veterans for Peace chapter wanted to come up with a stronger response to this new war. After a Veterans Day parade in November 2003, they began to think of organizing a way to mark the deaths of our soldiers, choosing a site on a beach in Santa Monica, California. At that time Ed told me that he felt pressure from the events of the new war and from his position as president of Veterans for Peace. He felt called upon to stand up more, "to find my voice," as he said, and to lead the group in a much stronger role. At the same time he felt uncomfortable and inadequate for the task. This strong feeling of lack and limitation stayed with him for quite a while, and when he heard of a vision-quest retreat I was organizing with entheogenic mushrooms, he signed up to participate. He said he considered these substances "holy sacraments."

The circle started out and we laid down, and for the next three hours I was uncomfortable and was not "getting off." I felt stuck. I attributed this to the linear consciousness I live in usually—I live in LA, run a business, am the parent of teen-agers. My intention was to get some direction in leading Veterans for Peace *and to find that inner voice that spoke my truth.*

I wasn't getting anywhere for three hours—and then it came and I was in the flow, as the side of the room on my left opened up into a scene of an army, an army from archaic times, a dark army of incredible power and evil. They rode past me—thousands—massive armies on horseback with armors, helmets, swords, shields, riding swiftly and with great momentum. There they were—the Hittites, the Parthians, the Achaeans, the Trojans, the Scythians. A masculine horde of death riding toward battle, they were out to kill and ravage—with the gnashing of teeth, the smiting of the enemy, they were determined killers, who represented all that was evil in these ancient masculine armies. I sat up in the room and I could see their leaders, those who sat up taller, with more colorful armor, helmets, plumes, larger horses, bigger swords. I pointed at these leaders and said 'Give me their power! Give me their power and I will use it for peace' (These words were not spoken out loud in the circle). I kept pointing and asking, as they kept riding by. I was completely in awe and filled with exhilaration and determination, and without fear as I saw this army of death.

Eventually this vision faded and I was in a cave by the ocean with ancient wise ones. I couldn't see them but I sensed their presence and they talked to me and told me of my responsibilities and what I needed to do, and of my commitment. They said I could always call on them and they would be my allies. After some time in the cave, this vision too faded and I was back in the room. When the talking stick was passed around I had some difficulty describing these visions—they were so powerful and life-like that I was nearly overcome.

After this experience, when Ed returned to Los Angeles, he and his friends from Veterans for Peace started to plan an Arlington West Memorial on the beach next to the Santa Monica Pier using white crosses, pictures, names, and signs. Ed and his friends Chuck and Mark were the principals, but others joined also, and they began putting the first crosses in the sand. They needed boards for the crosses, so people could write white cards with the soldiers' names on them and place them on the crosses. Ed wrote me as the ideas began to come through—he devised a system of boards to stand upright in the sand for the names. He found a website and downloaded all the names and pictures of veterans from Southern California who had been killed in various recent wars—at first 540, then 1,000. They made upright standing panels with all the pictures, so people could walk among them and see the photos. Ed wrote, "Almost with mania, I worked Saturdays and Sundays to build up the memorial. . . . I had a great flow of ideas from that vision. I made signs to explain various things to visitors about the memorial—our mission, how many had been killed, including how many Iraqis had been killed and so on. I don't remember ever in my life having such a passion for a project."

Fig. 9.1. Arlington West, Santa Monica, cemetery. Photo courtesy of Ed Ellis

Fig. 9.2. Ed Ellis at Arlington West, Santa Monica. Photo courtesy of Ed Ellis

In time, veterans and their families themselves visited the memorial and added personal mementos, photos, and flowers to the individual crosses. The project attracted considerable media attention. Looking back at this project, Ed wrote me in 2008, "I would be called on to speak publicly and I was hardly nervous, just allowing the words to come out, and people thanked me for speaking and I felt good about representing the Veterans for Peace group. I would joke with the reporters and look into their faces and tell the truth. Yes, it's nice to be recognized but more important and rewarding it has been to speak with the power of a peacemaker—guided by the ancients. I often think of that vision and call on it when I need to calm down before a speech. I sometimes stray and want to put it aside, but the vision pushes me and my life goes into imbalance unless I am working towards peace. Although I am no longer president of Veterans for Peace Los Angeles, I am still active and sought out by members to stay involved. The work goes on."

TEN

A HISTORY LESSON AT THE ÁCOMA PUEBLO

In September 2002, I had the opportunity to visit the Ácoma Pueblo, near Albuquerque, New Mexico, in the company of my friends Diane Haug and Roberto Weiss, during the Harvest Feast Day celebrations. We got there midmorning on a blazing hot day with a cloudless sky, and the Harvest Dance had been in progress for some hours already. In the following account, I interweave my own impressions on that day with selected passages about the history of the Ácoma Pueblo from a guidebook I had been reading—*Indian Villages of the Southwest,* by Buddy Mays.

> Perched atop a dramatic 365-foot-high, slab-sided sandstone mesa, Ácoma is appropriately called *Sky City.* Probably built around 900 A.D., it is one of the oldest occupied villages in the United States. The pueblo's initial contact with Europeans came in 1541 when Capt. Hernando de Alvarado and 20 Spanish soldiers stopped at the lofty village to demand supplies. . . . Alvarado reported that the village contained an estimated population of 6,000 and that the mesa's only access was a narrow path literally carved from the solid rock. For the next half century Ácoma was left alone by all save a few priests.

A long line of tightly linked dancers—men, women, and children— was moving with rhythmic steps through and around the plaza, between

Fig. 10.1. Ácoma Pueblo in the far right distance.
Photo by Scott Catron

Fig. 10.2. Ácoma Pueblo dwellings.
Photo by Scott Catron

and around the nearby houses, coiling back on itself like a giant serpent, so that sometimes two or three lines of dancers would be moving close by each other. A core group of four or five men drummers stood in the center of the plaza around one gigantic drum, keeping a vigorous beat going and chanting continuously. The sound of the drum dominated the atmosphere. All or most of the dancers had boughs of spruce tied to their arms and sometimes to their torsos as well. The women had little tablets tied to their hair on top of the head. On these tablets were painted images, like an ear of corn, a butterfly, or a bird. It occurred to me, though I do not know for sure, that perhaps these were the totemic emblems of the woman's family or clan.

The dancers' expressions were serious, relentlessly concentrated, with no extraneous movements or gestures. With their rhythmic dance steps on the ground, they were weaving the infinitely interconnected web of life through their community, the Earth, and the Spirit World. The dancing and chanting, we were told, was a prayer for rain. By midafternoon, clouds were spreading around the sky, and occasional raindrops were falling. There was some lightning and thunder in the distance to the west.

In 1598 Juan de Oñate, newly appointed governor of New Mexico, toured the pueblo. Later that same year, Oñate's nephew, Juan de Zaldívar, was sent to demand tribute and supplies. Fed up with Spanish extortion, Ácoma warriors attacked, and in a short ferocious battle Zaldívar and 13 of his soldiers were killed. The survivors quickly retreated. On January 12, 1599, Zaldívar's brother, Vicente, returned to the pueblo accompanied by 70 heavily armed men and demanded that the Indians responsible for the attack surrender. When no answer was forthcoming, Vicente Zaldívar placed the pueblo under siege and with a handful of men fought his way to the mesa top. Three days later, 800 Indians had been killed without a single Spanish loss. The Sky City was burned, and 600 captives were transported under guard to Santo Domingo Pueblo near the Rio Grande, to stand trial. The verdict: Guilty. All Ácoma men over

25 years of age were sentenced to 20 years in prison and the amputation of one foot. Elderly men and women were sold to friendly Plains Indians as slaves. Only children were released without punishment.

About 1603 Ácoma was rebuilt by surviving tribal members. A huge mission was constructed in 1629, using forced Indian labor under the dictatorial command of Spanish priests. When the pueblos revolted in 1680 the great mission was destroyed and the residing priest, Fray Lucas Maldonado, murdered. Not until 1699, long after most other pueblos had surrendered to the Spanish reconquest, did Ácoma finally capitulate and allow the priests to return and the mission to be rebuilt. Today, Ácoma is one of the friendliest of all the Southwestern pueblos.

I walked around with my friends Diane and Roberto, looking at the displays of arts and crafts set up at individual houses. We respectfully worked our way past and around the line of dancers and through the packed crowds of spectators. The dance, chants, and drumbeat were an audible and palpable presence everywhere and all the time, even when we were some yards away, walking between the buildings around tables displaying Ácoma pottery and woven cloth for sale. At one woman's little table, I was drawn to the pottery, with its distinctive designs, and I also noticed a piece of cloth hanging on the door, with similar designs on it. Possibly because the drumbeat and chanting were constantly in my ears and head, I suddenly got the impression that the designs on the pottery were a kind of musical notation of the chants. The hanging cloth with the designs looked like a music sheet. I asked the woman who was selling the pottery about this—whether the designs were related to the songs and chants. She gave me a strange, though not hostile, look and did not answer my question.

Ácoma artisans are best known for their black-on-white and black-and-red-on-white pottery. Most of the better ware is handmade in the village, then fired in traditional firing pits in the valley below, using cow dung as fuel. Ácoma pottery, usually elaborately decorated with

Fig. 10.3. An example of an Ácoma seed pot.

Fig. 10.4. Another example of Ácoma pottery

angular and curvilinear geometric designs, ranks among the most beautiful of all pueblo ceramics.

In the blazing heat of the afternoon, Diane and I went into the little church near the center of the plaza to cool off a bit. There were about a dozen tourists in the church. A local man, acting as a guide, started to relate some of the history of this pueblo—the massacres, the slave labor, the eight-year revolt of the enslaved Indians who took their sovereignty back. The church was built by Franciscan friars, using Indian slave labor. However, as our guide informed us, the workers secretly built sacred numbers and designs into the dimensions of the church without the Catholic priests ever knowing or suspecting. I thought to myself—this tour was getting more and more interesting. "The secret sacred designs made the church more acceptable to the Indians as a place of worship. We have two religions—the native and the Catholic—and they're integrated in this church," the guide explained.

Perhaps sensing our receptivity and interest, our guide spent some more time telling us of the pueblo's history. While maintaining their own beliefs and ceremonies in secret, the Indians learned to tolerate the presence of one priest in their village, who would do the rites of baptism, confirmation, and the like and conduct Sunday services for those who wanted to attend them. He said there was one time, however, in the nineteenth century, when the priest accidentally drowned an infant being baptized. Whereupon the adult men of the pueblo responded by throwing the priest off the cliff to the desert floor below.

Someone asked our guide if there was intermarriage between whites and Indians. He said yes, there was some, and then he launched into a long, detailed narrative about the differences between the native and Christian conception of marriage and the wedding rite. He said in the native tradition, at least in this pueblo, the woman chose the man she wanted to marry, and then he had to prove himself worthy of her choice. He did not elaborate on how the bridegroom was expected to prove himself worthy.

He then said he was going to show us the difference in the traditional wedding ceremony and asked Diane, who was sitting in a row by herself, if she would come up and let him demonstrate. She agreed and went up and stood next to him. He proceeded to describe the steps of the ceremony—what the bride says, what the groom says, and so forth, with the two of them standing side by side. Essentially he was going through a simulated wedding ceremony with Diane. All of us in the audience were totally absorbed and awed by this beautiful and eloquent ceremony, which was being performed in the cool, mostly empty church while the continuing drumming could still be heard outside.

After the guide had talked for a while, with great eloquence, he invited us to pose questions. I took the opportunity to again ask my question about the possible connection between the designs on the pottery and the notation of dance rhythms and melodies. He then launched into a commentary about his manner of talking, how he would sometimes talk very fast—and in fact his speech was getting faster as he said this—so that people wouldn't necessarily remember every detail. He said it was like stating your thought and then right away erasing the memory of the thought in your listeners. This was one of the advantages of an oral tradition, as theirs was: you could change the story as you told it according to the needs of the circumstances and the listeners. It remained fluid—whereas with writing, it becomes fixed. He talked on for several minutes, in a totally fascinating way, until it dawned on me that he hadn't answered my question and obviously had no intention of doing so. He had even erased my memory of having asked that question, at least for a while, and was explaining how he did that while he was doing it. By this time it did not matter to me anymore that my original question had been sidestepped, so to speak. I assumed this was an aspect of their culture that was secret to outsiders.

He was a Trickster storyteller, a word magician—deflecting my inquisitiveness and turning his speaking into a subtle and elegant teaching on the relationship between reality and the stories we tell ourselves and others. I was grateful for the teaching and thanked him as we walked out into the plaza, where a little rain was beginning to fall, and the sky was heavy with clouds. The dancers were continuing to snake around the houses, accompanied by the drumbeats and the chants of the men in the middle. The sounds remained in our minds for a long time as we climbed down from the Ácoma mesa and drove off.

ELEVEN

THE BROTHERS TERENCE
AND DENNIS MCKENNA

Reading the unique fraternal memoir *The Brotherhood of the Screaming Abyss* (2012), by Dennis McKenna, was both fascinating and moving for me. I was close friends with both the brothers, shared many stimulating conversations and psychedelic explorations with them, and was deeply saddened by Terence's early death in 2000 at the age of fifty-three. Terence became famous for his scintillating eloquence and Irish gift of the gab, like my old friend from an earlier generation, Timothy Leary. His provocative flights of the imagination, mixing far-out speculative science, radical politics, and arcane scholarship, delivered in his characteristic deadpan nasally inflected voice, astonished and delighted thousands—and remain circulating worldwide in disembodied recordings on the internet.

As his brother Dennis writes, "Terence channeled the *logos* of the age. Silver-tongued and a riveting speaker, he articulated the concepts that his fans groped for but could not express, and did so in a witty, disarming way. He was the gnomic trickster and bard, an elfin comedian delivering the cosmic punch line, even as he assured us we were all in on the cosmic joke" (McKenna 2012, 452). Especially, one might add, if you followed his advice and continued to take what he liked to call "heroic doses" of psychoactive mushrooms and DMT.

I first met Terence in the mid-1980s, when he gave a presentation at Arthur Young's Institute for the Study of Consciousness in Berkeley,

California. Arthur Young (1905–1995) was a mathematician, inventor, and cosmologist who had spent almost twenty years working with models for a helicopter design—eventually obtaining the first patent for the "wing-less flying device." After this he retired and devoted himself to his real interest, which was developing what he called a "comprehensive cosmology of process." The Arthur Young Institute was for several years a premier gathering place for the discussion of innovative ideas in many fields. Terence was at that time just emerging from the self-imposed public isolation necessitated by his career as a purveyor of high-quality psilocybin mushrooms for the underground market and launching his career as a public speaker. I did not know of his work with mushroom cultivation at that time, as I was in my post-Harvard and post-Millbrook phase of intentional distance from the world of psychedelics.

As Terence later told me, he felt that during the time he was an underground mushroom grower, his psyche was in a posture of paranoid isolation, like a clenched fist—concerned over the very real danger that the exposure of his activities could pose to himself and his young

Fig. 11.1. Terence with the *Psychotria viridis* plant, lower right (one of the ingredients of the ayahuasca brew) in Hawaii, 1987. Photo by Ralph Metzner

family. The paranoid fist started to unclench when he dismantled his lab and launched his career as a public speaker. His eloquence and creativity soared. When we met at the Arthur Young Institute, we agreed to get together and talk about our common interests in "excruciating detail," as he put it.

I started to visit the McKenna home in Sonoma County periodically, where we would engage in long, detailed, fascinating, and humorous conversations on language, history, psychedelics, cosmology, alchemy, esoteric literature, and our many shared interests and connections. Actually, our conversations were largely one-sided, since I was not used to consuming the large quantities of cannabis in various forms that seemed to be Terence's daily functional staple, so I mostly remained in a stoned receptive mode. Our friendship grew, and sometime after these initial contacts, I also met Dennis, who was at that time finishing up his doctoral work in plant biochemistry.

Fig. 11.2. Terence at one of the Palenque seminars in March 1999.
Photo by Ralph Metzner

I became aware of the work the McKenna brothers had done in inventing and describing a relatively simple process of growing psilocybin mushrooms from spores in glass jars—thereby making these mushrooms accessible to millions and obviating the plundering invasions of the mountains of Oaxaca by fungus-loving hippies. The *Psilocybin Magic Mushroom Growers Guide,* which the two published pseudonymously in 1976, is to my mind one of the most important contributions the brothers made to the advancement of culture. In the introduction to that little booklet is a passage that has the unmistakable imprint of Terence the cosmic visionary, channeling the species intelligence of the psilocybin mushroom.

I am old, older than thought in your species, which is itself fifty times older than your history. Though I have been on earth for ages, I am from the stars. My home is no one planet, for many worlds scattered through the shining disc of the galaxy have conditions which allow my spores an opportunity for life. The mushroom which you see is the part of my body given to sex thrills and sun bathing, my true body is a fine network of fibers growing through the soil. These networks may cover acres and may have far more connections than the number in a human brain. My mycelial network is nearly immortal—only the sudden toxification of a planet or the explosion of its parent star can wipe me out. By means impossible to explain because of certain misconceptions in your model of reality all my mycelial networks are in hyperlight communication across space and time. The mycelial body is as fragile as a spider's web but the collective hypermind and memory is a vast and historical archive of the career of evolving intelligence on many worlds in our spiral star swarm. Space, you see, is a vast ocean to those hardy life forms that have the ability to reproduce from spores, for spores are covered with the hardest organic substance known. Across the aeons of time and space drift many spore-forming life-forms in suspended animation for millions of years until contact is made with a suitable environment. Few such species are minded, only myself and my recently evolved near relatives have achieved the hyper-communication mode and memory capacity that makes us leading members in the community of galactic intelligence. How the hyper-communication mode operates is a secret which will not be lightly given to man. But the means should be obvious: it is the occurrence of psilocybin and psilocin in the biosynthetic pathways of my living body that opens for me and my symbiots the vision screens to many worlds. You as an individual and man as a species are on the brink of the formation of a symbiotic relationship with my genetic material that will eventually carry humanity and earth into the galactic mainstream of the higher civilizations.

Since it is not easy for you to recognize other varieties of intelligence around you, your most advanced theories of politics and society have advanced only as far as the notion of collectivism. But beyond the cohesion of the members of a species into a single organism there lie richer and even more baroque evolutionary possibilities. Symbiosis is one of these. Symbiosis is a relation of mutual dependence and positive benefits for both of the species involved. Symbiotic relationships between myself and civilized forms of higher animals have been established many times and in many places throughout the long ages of my development. These relationships have been mutually useful; within my memory is the knowledge of hyperlight drive ships and how to build them. I will trade this knowledge for a free ticket to new worlds around suns younger and more stable than your own. To secure an eternal existence down the long river of cosmic time I again and again offer this agreement to higher beings and thereby have spread throughout the galaxy over the long millennia. A mycelial network has no organs to move the world, no hands; but higher animals with manipulative abilities can become partners with the star knowledge within me and if they act in good faith, return both themselves and their humble mushroom teacher to the million worlds to which all citizens of our star swarm are heir. (Oss and Oeric 1976, 8–9)

Dennis, who was close to and admired his eloquent and imaginative older brother, took on a different role in society after the two intrepid explorers returned from the shamanic-alchemical-cosmic *folie à deux* described in their coauthored autobiography *The Invisible Landscape* (1975) as "the experiment at La Chorrera" (discussed below). Dennis went back to school, got a Ph.D. in plant biochemistry, and embarked on a career as research scientist in botanical medicine. His writing in *The Brotherhood of the Screaming Abyss* (2012) autobiography is enormously engaging—brilliantly articulating complex issues of natural history while dealing honestly and humbly with the personal, familial, and professional challenges that had confronted him.

Terence once commented to me that while he was known as the more eloquent speaker and storyteller, his brother Dennis was, in his view, the more profound thinker and scientist. "His mind goes deep into matter," he said with obvious admiration. Indeed Dennis carved out a significant career as a consultant in the development of new botanical medicines, with a slew of research publications to his credit. I've always loved listening to his lucid and articulate explanations of complex concepts in molecular biology and ethnobotany.

To my mind, one of the most absorbing passages in Dennis's autobiography is in the chapter where he describes the research work he and two colleagues—Charles Grob, M.D., and J. C. Callaway, Ph.D.—did on the chemistry and psychopharmacology of ayahuasca for the Brazilian Uniao de Vegetal (UDV) church. Their work resulted in several scientific papers published in the botanical and pharmacological literature. In 1991, the UDV had organized a scientific medical conference in São Paulo at which the three North American scientists presented their research, as did the Brazilian scientists and medical doctors associated with the church. I was also invited to present at the conference, as were the Colombian anthropologist Luis Eduardo Luna and the independent pharmacognosist Jonathan Ott.

During the conference, the six of us primarily English-speaking friends met also for less formal get-togethers. I remember in one of these, stimulated by the consumption of some high-grade local cannabis, we were sitting in a loose circle, all seemingly talking and listening intently at the same time. Whether any of us could recall anything that we talked about is another matter. In this kind of get-together it seems to be the convivial sharing that is important, not the content of what is said.

Since the UDV is both a scientific and medical research organization and an ayahuasca-using church, a ceremony was organized following the conference. Several hundred people from the UDV church attended this ceremony, which was of course held in Portuguese, though some translators were provided for the English-speaking attendees. It was during this ceremony, after consuming a concoction of the visionary vine, that Dennis found himself subjectively identified as a sentient

Fig. 11.3. Back row: Jonathan Ott, Charles Grob. Front row: Dennis McKenna, J. C. Callaway, Ralph Metzner at the International Hoasca Conference in Rio de Janeiro, 1995. Photo from Ralph Metzner's collection

Fig. 11.4. Dennis McKenna, Ralph Metzner, and Tom Manning at the International Hoasca Conference in Rio de Janeiro, 1995. Photo from Ralph Metzner's collection

water molecule and was shown and actually experienced the entire process of photosynthesis step by step. As a plant biochemist, he was able to name the different biochemical processes he had come to understand *objectively,* as he was now experiencing them *subjectively,* from the point of view of a single drop of water landing on a leaf and initiating the processes of photosynthesis. The following are two small selections, from the beginning and the end, of his brilliantly articulated scientific translation of the core biochemical process of life on planet Earth.

(1) Somehow I understood—though no words were involved—that the *Banisteriopsis* vine was the embodiment of the plant intelligence that embraced and covered the earth, that together the community of the plant species that existed on the earth providing the nurturing energy that made life on earth possible. I "understood" that photosynthesis—that neat trick, known only to green plants, of making complex organic compounds from sunlight, carbon dioxide and water . . . was the force on which all life depends.

I found myself transported from my bodiless perch in space to the lightless depths beneath the surface of the earth. I had somehow become a sentient water molecule, percolating randomly through the soil, lost amid the tangle of the enormous fibers of the *Banisteriopsis* world tree. . . .

I recognized that I had entered the first phases of the pentose phosphate shunt, the biochemical pathway that builds the initial products of photosynthesis into complex sugars and sends them spinning from thence into the myriad pathways of biosynthesis that ultimately generate the molecular stuff of life. . . .

(2) I felt humbled, shaken, exhausted and exalted all at the same time. Suddenly, I was ripped out of my molecular roller coast ride and my disembodied eye was suspended high over the Amazon basin. . . . The day was sunny, the vista stretching to the curved horizon was blue and green and bluish-green, the vegetation below, threaded with shining rivers, looked like green mold covering an overgrown petri plate. I was wracked with a sense of overwhelming sadness mixed with fear for the delicate balance of life on this planet, the fragile processes that drive and sustain life, sadness for the fate of the planet and its precious cargo. . . .

Suddenly, again from behind my left shoulder, came a quiet voice. "You monkeys only *think* you are running things," it said. "You don't think we would really allow this to happen, do you?" And somehow, I knew that the "we" in that statement was the entire community of species that constitute the planetary biosphere. I knew that I had been given an inestimable gift, a piece of gnosis and wisdom straight from the heart-mind of planetary intelligence, conveyed in visions and thought by an infinitely wise, incredibly ancient, and enormously compassionate "ambassador" to the human community. (McKenna 2012, 435–9)

This was a core vision of Dennis's life work as a scientist, presaging a time in our civilization when the external observations and measurements of natural scientists could be supplemented by the interior observations of those same scientists in sensitized and enhanced states of consciousness. While Terence's core vision was the connection with fungal intelligence on a macrocosmic scale, Dennis's connection was with the microcosmic molecular web of planetary plant intelligence.

In his fraternal autobiography, Dennis is frank about the unusual degree of closeness of the two brothers, surely triggered by the death of their mother when they were in their early twenties, and fueled by the daily consumption of huge amounts of cannabis, as they made their 1960s migration from small-town Colorado to the West Coast hippie carnival. In 1971, the brothers, young men in their twenties, ventured on a journey to Colombia, together with several friends, to search for ayahuasca, the legendary shamanic hallucinogen, which was relatively unknown at that time. What they found, unexpectedly, were large quantities of high-potency psilocybin mushrooms, with which they began what they called "the experiment at La Chorrera." This was described in their coauthored 1975 book *The Invisible Landscape*.

Basically, the experiment consisted of both of them repeatedly ingesting large quantities of the mushrooms, listening to a kind of interior, alien-sounding, buzzing or humming sound, and then reproducing that sound vocally. The purpose, as they conceived it, was to induce a lasting expanded state of consciousness. They had a complex theory, which they were discussing and elaborating in intense daily speculative conversations, of how the psilocybin could activate endogenous tryptamines in the brain and create some kind of "holo-cybernetic unit of superconductive genetic material, activated via tryptamine harmonic interference."

Following the ingestion of an enormous dose of nineteen psilocybin mushrooms (a normal dose being perhaps three to six), plus continuous smoking of cannabis and also consuming some ayahuasca that Terence had brewed up, and experimenting with prolonged vocal ululations, Dennis developed a thought-hallucination, sympathetically supported by Terence, in which he felt they both were in touch with a "Teacher" of some kind. This Teacher would guide them, as Dennis related, to "generate a hologram, which would begin to broadcast the information stored in the DNA, making the data both comprehensible to thought and open to manipulation by thought. If the experiment worked, one of us in the near vicinity would be turned into a DNA radio, transmitting the collective knowledge of all earthly life, all the time" (McKenna 2012, 252).

While Dennis was being flooded by these eschatological thought-hallucinations and furiously scribbling notes about the information he was downloading, Terence was playing the supportive role of maintaining contact and communication, while resisting the urgings of their companions to commit his brother to a mental institution. Dennis wrote:

> In retrospect, I see how our conceits embodied a paradox of psychedelic experience. . . . On one level we understood that a molecule doesn't contain the trip. Rather, the trip is an interaction between a living organism and the molecule's pharmacological properties. Those properties may be inherent to the drug, but the trip itself is not. . . . We got that, sort of. But in our delusion, if that's what it was, we also embraced a conflicting view: We believed an intelligent entity resided in the drug, or at least somehow communicated to us through it. Even as we theorized about the 4-D expression of the drug—that the trip could somehow be expressed on its exterior by rotation through the fourth dimension—we were assuming on another level that a being of some sort was directing the trip. We weren't the first or the last to make that "mistake." After all, this is very close to shamanistic views of psychedelic experience, in which the drug speaks through a skilled practitioner. (McKenna 2012, 247)

Here, I believe, was a crucial turning point in the development of their shared delusion, which was due to the brothers' inevitable conditioning and commitment to the materialist worldview, as children of their time and their world. In the shamanistic worldview, the visions do not come from the drug or the plant, nor even from the shaman guide who speaks or sings—whom the two brothers in any event did not have. The visions come from the *spirits* associated with the plants or fungi, who communicate with the shamanic practitioner or explorer. The shaman traditionally has established relationships with specific plant and animal spirits and is thus able to decode the messages and visions "coming through" (or "being downloaded") and can translate them into the locally appropriate action or teaching.

As a scientific materialist in good standing with his profession, Dennis, in his autobiography, offers his support of the reductionist credo, though he clearly has some reservations:

> These substances did none of these things. The human mind-brain created these experiences. At La Chorrera, the psilocybin somehow triggered metabolic processes that caused a part of our brains to be experienced not as part of the self, but as the "other"—a separate, intelligent entity that seemed to be downloading a great many peculiar ideas into our consciousness. That's the reductionist perspective. Is it true? I honestly can't say, even today. If either is true, or if the alternative true, that there are actually entities in hyperspace that can communicate with us via something akin to telepathy when the brain is affected by large amount of tryptamine—that's a hypothesis worth testing, if such an experiment could ever be devised. (McKenna 2012, 248)

From my own perspective, having long ago abandoned the reductionism of modern science and become a radical empiricist in the sense of William James, I would say that one needs to first simply *describe the experiences*—and only later, and separately, speculate about their meanings and implications for our existing worldview. Easier said than done, considering the irrepressible excitement of new discoveries. You have to hold the theoretical speculations in abeyance until the intensity of the experiential download diminishes somewhat, and you can calmly reflect on the experience.

Certainly by now there are numerous individuals in the psychedelic shamanic subculture who have had multiple experiences of intelligent communications with spirits, and who have learned, with practice, to decipher such communications and utilize them in their projects of healing or creative expression. In the early 1970s, however, these two young explorers from Colorado were just beginning their lifelong journeys as psychonauts.

Over the years, I have been around dozens of people, myself included, who, as a result of ill-prepared ingestion of high-dose psychedelics, got temporarily caught in a delusional thought system. They may have profound insights, but tend to overgeneralize their significance. Delusions of grandeur are mixed with genuine amazement at the bewildering magnificence of the actual world of nature around us and within us. Following are some examples of such delusional overgeneralization in the text that Dennis wrote while he was setting himself up for the high-dose experiment (McKenna 2012, 253–4).

"In the final Stone the tryptamines act as a superconductive antenna to pick up on all cosmic energy in space and time."

Not just picking up *some* cosmic energy, but *all*.

"It will constitute the 4-D holographic memory of the device, and will contain and explicate the genetic history of all species."

As if picking up the genetic history of one species or even one individual wouldn't be significant enough!

Overgeneralization is an aspect of the delusions of grandeur—perhaps a special feature of high-dose psychedelic drug experiences. At our communal experiment in Millbrook in the early 1960s, I recall many times being cornered by a wild-eyed hippie wanting to impart the ultimate cosmic secret he had just been granted on his trip, a secret he was sure everyone would appreciate for its earth-shattering profundity. Receiving such visions does seem of overwhelming importance, *and it is*—to the individual concerned. Others, like family members or professionals, may not appreciate the vision's cosmic significance and are more likely to be alarmed by the tenuous nature of the individual's connections to ordinary reality. Visionaries are notorious for appearing to others like madmen.

As a psychologist, I do not consider that what Dennis experienced was a kind of schizophrenia or psychosis. Schizophrenia is characterized by fragmented ideation, flattened affect, and the inability to think rationally. What Dennis experienced was a profoundly unusual fragmentation of thought processes, accompanied by the true memory-knowledge that he was in an altered state triggered by the intentional consumption of a high dose of visionary mushrooms. The situation would be entirely different for those poor souls who, having ignorantly or inadvertently ingested psychoactive drugs, find themselves with fragmented perceptions of internal and external realities—with no reassuring knowledge that this was a temporary state and with no personal support system. Psychotic-like experiences can and do sometimes occur with unprepared, unguided, and unprotected ingestion of psychoactive drugs or substances. In the contemporary era of Burning Man festivals, there are subcultural knowledge systems and practices for intervening safely and effectively in psychotic or delusional drug trips. But this knowledge did not exist when the McKenna brothers were on their explorations.

From my present perspective, I would say that the McKenna brothers experienced a glimpse into what shamans call the *spirit world* and what the brothers themselves later called "hyperspace." They were intuitively groping for new terminology to describe their new experiences and integrate them into their worldview of that time. There actually *is* an inexhaustible vastness of other dimensions in our universe. They are always there, but are only accessible in visionary states of consciousness, or near-death experiences, or through shamanic practices or dreams, or, alternatively, through observation technologies like microscopes and telescopes. The mystical literature of all times and cultures is replete with paradoxical descriptions of the grandeur of the hitherto unperceived and unimagined. The unwritten lore of shamans and visionaries has many examples of knowledge seekers who at some point in their initiatory process lost their way and became temporarily deranged before finding their true life path.

Yes, their glimpse was fragmentary, and yes, they were unprepared, and yes, they had no ready-made language to describe what they found. Visions of nonordinary realities can only be communicated if one has access to a worldview and a consensual language to describe them. The brothers did not have either at the time of their "experiment." Since that time, they have both contributed significantly to creating an expanded worldview—Terence through his imaginative and inspiring cosmological speculations, Dennis through his solid scientific investigations into ethnobotanical medicines and their neurochemical effects.

Reflecting on his experiences of forty years before, the sixty-year-old Dennis writes poignantly about the wild misadventure of his twenty-year-old former self.

The ravings of a madman, I'll grant you that. And yet, there is also poetry here, and beauty, and a longing for redemption. What I expressed is not that different from the vision articulated by the most compassionate and beautiful of the world's religions: the universe will not achieve perfection until all beings have achieved enlightenment. Isn't that what I'm saying? No doubt there is messianic delusion here; indeed, in passages a bit further on in that text I discuss my role as cosmic Antichrist. But there is also a deep wish for healing, not only of myself but of the universe. Our mother had been dead less than six months. I have to believe that much of what happened to us at La Chorrera was linked to that tragic event. So overwhelmed were we by the sense of loss, and of guilt, we were ready to tear space and time apart in order to reverse that cosmic injustice. (McKenna 2012, 257)

Over the next couple of weeks, Dennis put his fragmented identity programs back into a functional order while Terence was obsessively starting to construct his own metaphysical system, which later became known as Time Wave Zero. The brothers' companions, who could see only incipient psychosis, wanted to bring Dennis to a psychiatric facility—no small task considering they were in the Amazon jungle. Dennis writes that he remains "grateful to Terence for resisting the pressure to leave La Chorrera. He insisted that whatever was happening to us be allowed to unfold in its own time and on its own terms—there was no need for intervention beyond making sure that I didn't wander off or hurt myself."

Terence's intuitive understanding of the need to let the fragmented self-system of his brother find its own way back to center and to wholeness was and is consonant with the teachings of psychiatrists like Ronald Laing, Stanislav Grof, John Perry, and others who have championed the idea that some forms of so-called psychosis can best be understood as the psyche's own natural healing journey—a process that should be supported by others and not cut short by psychiatric medications or hospitalization. In this view, a supportive and benevolent attitude toward psychotic self-delusions is considered therapeutic and is particularly appropriate when the apparent break in reality perception has been triggered by a drug experience.

In an essay published in his book *The Archaic Revival,* Terence returned to elaborate on the theme of the extraterrestrial origin of the hallucinogenic mushrooms.

The mushroom was a species that did not evolve on Earth. Within the mushroom trance I was informed that once a culture has complete understanding of its genetic information, it reengineers itself for survival. The *Stropharia cubensis* mushroom's version of reengineering is a mycelial network strategy when in contact with planetary surfaces and spore-dispersion strategy as a means of radiating throughout the galaxy. . . . The other side does seem to be in possession of a huge body of information drawn from the history of the galaxy. . . . The *Stropharia cubensis* mushroom, if one can believe what it says in one of its moods, is a symbiote, and it desires ever deeper symbiosis with the human species. It achieved symbiosis with human society early by associating itself with domesticated cattle and through them human nomads. (McKenna 1991, 39)

He cheerfully goes on to argue against his own thesis of extraterrestrial origin though, when he goes on to say: "I've recently come to suspect that the human soul is so alienated from our present culture that we treat it as an extraterrestrial. To us the most alien thing in the cosmos is the human soul" (McKenna 1991, 40).

In another essay published in *The Archaic Revival,* Terence continues to speculate, perhaps reluctantly, about the connection between psilocybin mushroom visions of UFOs and actual ET contacts.

We have ascertained by questionnaire that UFO contact is perhaps the motif most frequently mentioned by people who take psilocybin recreationally, using doses sufficient to elicit the full spectrum of psychedelic effects. They encounter another space with UFOs and aliens—classic little green men. DMT is similar. It also conveys one into wild, zany, elf-infested spaces. It's as though there were an alternative reality, linguistically as well as dimensionally. (McKenna 1991, 62)

I personally find this thesis—that extraterrestrial beings of superior intelligence who might be communicating or even symbiotically coevolving with the human species on Earth via entheogenic fungi and plants—plausible and certainly worthy of further investigation. It is consistent with the fact that interest in UFOs and extraterrestrial culture and contact has been growing tremendously in the last forty years, along with interest in consciousness expansion through psyche-delics, shamanism, and spiritual practices. The notion that experiences with Amazonian hallucinogenic vines and mushrooms could facilitate or induce visions of extraterrestrial visitors and spaceships is richly sup-ported by the art of Pablo Amaringo, a Peruvian *ayahuasquero* who painted hundreds of visionary experiences, including many encounters with extraterrestrial beings and flying craft (Amaringo and Luna 1991).

In conversations with Terence during the 1990s, I sometimes broached the question of extraterrestrial contact during experiences with hallucinogens. I mentioned the work of my colleague and friend, the Harvard psychiatrist John Mack (1929–2004), who made an exten-sive study of UFO contact and abduction experiences. Mack pointed out in his last book, *Passport to the Cosmos* (1999), that reported contact and communication with alien intelligences and extraterrestrial craft is widespread and taken for granted in societies with living shamanic tra-ditions, such as in South Africa and South America.

I pointed out to Terence that the "self-transforming machine elves" he describes as typical hallucinogenic mushroom "entities" resemble the descriptions of the "small greys" in the abduction literature. In his book *Abduction* (1994), Mack summarizes the hundreds of reports he has seen that describe the greys: "The small greys have large pear-shaped heads that protrude in the back, long arms with three or four long fingers, a thin torso and spindly feet." It seems to me that this description also could apply to the form of some mushrooms. In some reports it is explicitly claimed that the "greys" are semiautonomous robots—which reminded me of Terence's description of "self-transforming machine elves."

For whatever reason, Terence did not seem to appreciate the possi-bility I raised, that the "machine elves" he saw during some mushroom experiences were not necessarily associated with the mushrooms, but rather that they *only became visible* to him during states of expanded consciousness induced by hallucinogenic mushrooms. Others, myself included, have perceived various living and autonomous extraterrestrial entities without taking mushrooms or any psychedelic substance, for example in lucid dreams. And others, myself included, have had personal experiences with hallucinogenic mushrooms that did not include such machine elves, but a large variety of different kinds of spirit beings.

Terence McKenna's thesis on the symbiotic evolutionary role of entheogenic fungi was further extended in his major work, *Food of the Gods* (1992), in which he proposed that the discovery of consciousness-expanding mushrooms by our hominid ancestors might have led to the development of language, higher intelligence, and culture. While this thesis has generally been disdained or ignored by the academic establishment, there isn't really a good alternative theory for the development of language and higher intelligence other than that it is somehow associated with brain size.

More importantly, establishment academics who are not personally familiar with psychedelic experiences are not really in a position to evaluate McKenna's hypothesis appropriately. We can all recognize that scientists who have not looked through a microscope or a telescope are not qualified to evaluate the observations of those who have. This is the epistemological principle that William James called *radical empiricism* and the Dalai Lama has referred to as *first-person empiricism*.

Food of the Gods ranges far and wide through history and anthropology in its review of sacred mind-expanding substances. Terence reexamines R. G. Wasson's hypothesis that *soma,* a mysterious substance revered as a deity in the Vedas, was basically the fly agaric (*Amanita muscaria*) mushroom, imported from Central Asia. The historian of religion Mircea Eliade, who wrote a masterful scholarly overview of shamanism, considered the use of psychoactive plants a degenerate form of religious practice. Wasson, on the basis of his experiences in Mexico with the psilocybin mushroom and his beliefs about *soma,* took the opposite view. Wasson held that all religious experience had originally been induced by psychoactive plants or fungi and that the practices of yoga developed in India were substitute methods, created when the mushroom was no longer available to the ecstatic visionaries. Terence comes down on the side of Wasson, but thinks *soma* was a psilocybin mushroom, not the fly agaric, on the grounds that the latter is only mildly and ambiguously hallucinogenic. In any case, apart from some apparently mushroom-shaped carved stones, no evidence has been found for either mushroom species existing in India.

It may never be possible to settle this question in the history of religious practices completely. But that psychedelic or hallucinogenic plants or fungi may have played a role in the origins of *some* religious traditions, as well as some aspects of language (for example, bardic poetry) seems to me both plausible and probable.

———

Postscript 2011. During the past twenty years there has been an enormous increase of interest in shamanic enthogens, especially ayahuasca. Hundreds, if not thousands, of middle-class, urban Westerners have made pilgrimages to the Amazon region in search of ayahuasca guides. Many books have been written and documentaries made about ayahuasca, to show the indigenous context as well as something of the extraordinary visual content of the experience and to discuss its implications. After seeing one of these documentaries I initiated a correspondence with Dennis McKenna. The following conversations by email took place while he was writing his fraternal autobiography, *The Brotherhood of the Screaming Abyss.*

RALPH: Hi, Dennis. I just saw this film, *Vine of the Soul,* in which you are a featured speaker. It was shown at the Institute of Noetic Sciences (IONS) in a new film series that IONS was doing, in which I was asked to be a discussant. The audience all wanted to see the five or six extra portions of the interview with you. Everyone was very impressed by the things you said, as I was. I asked—and found out—that about four-fifths of the audience had personally experienced ayahuasca. So the film's narration of the ayahuasca experience wasn't particularly new or revelatory to the audience. But your explanations of the science and your evolutionary speculations were gripping. Some of the time I got the impression you were almost "channeling" Terence—you sounded sort of like him. But at other times in the interview you were speaking in your own voice as a true scientist-explorer who seeks to understand and express both objective and the subjective perspectives on our multi-dimensional world.

In fact, at one point in the film you said something that I didn't quite catch, so I wanted to ask you about it: you said *something is to something as mass is to gravity* (in other words it was a relational analogy). Was it—*consciousness is to life*—*as mass is to gravity*? This seemed to me like a gem of insight.

It occurs to me that I hope you can structure the book you're writing about Terence and his ideas in such a way that it expresses what ideas and insights you yourself have brought through, and developed further, stimulated no doubt by his words. It is like you both were exploring two different but overlapping and related branches from the tree of infinite knowledge. I remember Terence saying one day early in the history of our friendship—and you weren't in on that particular conversation—that while he was the more eloquent and elegant speaker and communicator, you were the true scientist who penetrated deep into matter. Now it seems you're acquiring something of his skill as a communicator too. And maybe you'll continue channeling Terence.

DENNIS: Hi Ralph. Thanks for the compliments and your very kind words. I never really know how my words come out sounding to others—and as you well know, sometimes you're "on" and sometimes you're not. With the interview for that film, I felt like I was "on"; so it's confirming to hear that other people liked it too. Whether I'm channeling Terence, that's a very hard thing to know. Sometimes I feel like I am; at other times it's clear that I'm not channeling him, but whatever is coming is from a similar "place" that he was able to tap into at will. At other times, it's clearly just me. So I don't know about the channeling thing. What's weird about it for me is that we were so close when T was alive, and our ideas were complementary but not identical, it was almost like we were expressing right-brain and left-brain mirrors of each other—we each had half of the total picture.

But in day to day life, I don't feel like I "channel" Terence exactly, it's more like he's just always there. We conduct conversations in my head all the time, so it seems quite natural. I know him or knew him so well, I can speak both in his voice and in my own. Of course this has to be a delusion, but it still seems this way. I enjoy having him kind of constantly present, like a silent partner. Things come up and I just know how he would react. I suppose a psychotherapist might say this is a serious problem and I should really get therapy to step out from under his shadow. But you know, I kind of like having him around! He was always a great conversationalist and so there is always someone interesting to talk to.

RALPH: With regard to your relationship with Terence: I tend to think that it doesn't really matter who channels who. Ideas are and should be tested and validated by the observations and commentaries of others. One of my teachers used to say we're always being guided, taught, and inspired by various spirit-beings, some known to us, some not. I remember once having a flash of insight that came to me in a voice and in words that sounded just like Buckminster Fuller—and I had been attending a workshop where he talked for hours.

DENNIS: This is an interesting idea, and not so strange to those who know the shamanic dimensions from experience. There does seem to be some realm, "out there" or "in here" or somewhere, that is populated with entities of all kinds; some are wise counselors and teachers, others are malevolent. But are these entities "real" in an objective sense, or are they parts of our own brain/mind, parts of our consciousness that have somehow "split off" from our main conscious identity and present themselves as autonomous? Isn't this what having multiple personalities would be like? I don't have any answers of course. You tell me, you're the psychologist!

RALPH: I don't agree when you say, referring to your postmortem conversations with Terence, "Of course this has to be a delusion." When you describe how sometimes you are thinking or speaking sometimes with Terence's voice and sometimes your own—that sounds perfectly natural to me and, speaking as a psychologist, "normal." You wouldn't want to pre-screen your inner conversations with your brother as delusional—when instead they might be inspirational. After all, it matters not where our ideas come from, but what we do with them when we receive them. That's the empirical attitude and method. I also don't agree at all that you need psychotherapy to get out of Terence's shadow. Your sibling relationship has always seemed to be primarily supportive and positive, both before and after his death.

DENNIS: More to the point of what I alluded to above: Whether these "entities," teachers, or whatever are objectively real or not doesn't really matter. Is anything objectively real, given that the brain basically synthesizes a "reality hallucination" in which we are always immersed? If the "entities" present information, insights, understandings that seem to be valid, then it doesn't really matter if they are "real" or not. The trick is, how do you determine if they are valid? I think this is the knife edge between science, which seeks testability of hypotheses, and faith, which just pretty much accepts assertions about reality without applying any tests, the information is presumed to be valid because of the presumed source.

RALPH: Exactly; I agree completely. With regard to the extremely interesting question about consciousness we were discussing, you were saying: "consciousness is an emergent property of complexity as gravity is an emergent property of mass." And I thought you said, or heard you saying: "consciousness relates to life as mass relates to gravity." So it seems to me that we may be on to something here.

DENNIS: With regard to the analogy I used in the documentary, what I said was a metaphor I've often used in public discourses, and it is that consciousness is an emergent property of complexity, just as gravity is an emergent property of mass. Get enough mass stuffed inside a critical radius and strange things start to happen, like the formation of black holes and the singularity that goes with that. By analogy, the human brain is the most complex object in the known universe, and seems somehow to be intimately tied to consciousness (although I don't necessarily think the brain generates all consciousness). But by analogy, if you get enough biological complexity stuffed into a critical radius, like a human skull, the emergent quality of consciousness becomes overtly manifest. It's always present in matter to some extent but only becomes obvious in highly complex organized structures. Or something like that. Anyway it was a good rap.

RALPH: Indeed! Gravity as an "emergent property of mass"—is that a standard view in physics, or is that something you channeled?

DENNIS: Yes, I think it is the standard view. If I'm channeling, I'm channeling Einstein, who said that gravity was really a property of space-time, the curvature in space-time produced by mass. If you get enough mass into a small enough radius (the so-called *Schwarzschild* radius) then strange things happen—mainly, space-time completely wraps around itself and you get a black hole. Think of it as poking a depression in an elastic rubber sheet and then twisting it off to form a separate bubble. Inside that bubble is a *singularity*, a region where the normal laws of physics may not apply, and you can't say anything about it or make any measurements because it's totally outside the continuum. You can only infer what's going on inside the singularity by making measurements close to the event horizon. When you get a critical amount of complexity stuffed into a small enough space, like a human cranium, then you get what amounts to a singularity. This is the totally simplistic layman's understanding, I have no idea of the math behind it.

But I liked the analogy: the brain is the most complex system we know, and as complexity increases in living systems, they display *emergent properties* like consciousness. All living things are conscious to some extent and they seem to be more conscious the more complex they are. Actually, being an animist I'd go further and assert that consciousness is an inherent property of being, perhaps even more fundamental than matter. This may be one reason why consciousness is so hard to nail down for the neuroscientists; you can't see or measure it directly, you can only infer its existence from external observations. Though of course we subjectively experience consciousness all the time, but that doesn't count! Another interesting speculation: maybe the singularity of physics and the singularity of complexity are one and the same. A singularity is by definition something you can't measure or make any supposition about; so it could be anything.

RALPH: Animism rocks! *Of course* everything is alive and consciousness all-pervasive! You're the self-described animist-scientist. Albert Hofmann was the self-described mystic-scientist. You're in good company.

———

Postscript 2014. As I was preparing this essay, I initiated some further correspondence and conversation with Dennis, to follow up on some tantalizingly incomplete memories I had of conversations with Terence concerning UFOs and ETs.

RALPH: Hi, Dennis—it's me again. I'm writing now to ask you whether you ever experienced or had any discussion with your brother about UFOs and ETs. During the seminars in Palenque, at all of which Terence was present all the time and I only some, the topic of UFO sightings and ET contacts came up—actually, I brought it up. I'd been reading John Mack's books and become friends with him, and was very impressed with the observations he and others have compiled. I have a memory of Terence often talking about the alien nature of mushroom experiences. In fact, his description of the "self-transforming machine elves" resembles to a remarkable degree the description of the "small greys" that Mack and others have identified as one particular species of off-world visitors: three- to four-feet tall grey-skinned beings with huge eyes and elongated heads, that seem to be able to reach into and control the minds and bodies of the contactees or abductees. They are the most widely reported off-world species in the ET literature. Some say they are from Zeta Reticuli, here by secret agreement to do some genetic experiments with human-alien hybrid breeding. I was struck in the similarity between Terence's described "machine elves" and the "small greys." In some of the ET literature they are described as part living, part robot.

When I brought up this question in a seminar discussion in which Terence and I were both speakers, he dismissed the idea and made sarcastic jokes about people's fantasies of sex and breeding with aliens. I sensed that it was somehow threatening to him to consider this possibility—he seemed to prefer his own fantastic language of "self-transforming machine elves" that were somehow associated with mushrooms. My alternative hypothesis was that the mushrooms may have expanded Terence's perceptual systems in some instances, so that he could "see" these beings, which others have also seen, even without mushrooms. I didn't get the sense that he was an abductee, but that maybe the greys or other aliens had become perceptible to him at times when he'd taken the mushrooms and his perception was sensitized.

My question to you now is whether you and your brother in your conversations ever talked about possible ET contacts or visions either one of you had had in the past. I have a vague memory of Terence saying at one point that either you or he or both of you saw a UFO when you were kids, maybe preteens or thereabouts. So my question is basically whether this question triggers any memories of your own experience in this regard, and whether you remember any conversations with Terence about it. I hope it isn't painful for you to be asked to remember your childhood and later experiences with Terence.

DENNIS: Hi Ralph, good to hear from you, as always! Your questions are not painful, but they are difficult to answer because I'm trying to cast my mind back many decades, and I don't need hypnotic amnesia from alien greys to make my memories foggy. I'm perfectly capable of doing that myself!

I never heard Terence or anyone else, besides you, compare the "machine elves" to the greys. I'm not sure I've ever seen machine elves on tryptamines, and I'm pretty sure I never saw greys on or off tryptamines; if I did I have no recollection of those encounters. I don't think Terence saw any similarity between MEs [machine elves] and greys. The greys, in the classic UFO reports, are definitely creatures, humanoid, diminutive, sometimes seeming quite sinister, sometimes otherwise. They might share with the "machine elves" elements of mischievousness; and maybe that they were part machine and part biological, but I think the resemblance ends there.

The "machine elves" became for Terence a glib way to refer to the entities that he encountered, and to talk about them without having to explain every time what he meant. The term became a *gestalt* for something that he couldn't really comprehend, and that was kind of the point—they were not describable. Once that notion became constellated he used it as a convenient rubric, and others picked up on it as well. But clearly his concept is that these things were partly autonomous intelligences of some kind, they were made of information, and they were constantly transforming in shape and appearance. They did not present as "elves" or humanoids in shape; but they were "elfin" in that they were joyous, humorous, clownish. They bounced around and were so delighted when he "showed up" in their space (dimension, cosmic circus or whatever it was).

What is also not clear to me is whether the "machine elves" were a constant feature of his DMT experiences. Did they show up every time, or only occasionally, or maybe only the first time? So I don't think Terence would agree with your view that the "machine elves" and the greys are the same, or even similar. Both appear to be intelligent non-human entities, but also both could be confabulations of the mind or parts of the self presenting as non-self. The fact that high doses of

DMT can in some people elicit an "abduction" experience would argue for this. If you're on a hospital bed hooked up to IV DMT and you have an abduction experience, or you have a similar experience alone on a lonely road in Arizona, what does that say about the experience? I'm not sure but it suggests to me that it's something that your mind creates. Either that or there really is another dimension "out there" and portals to that dimension can open up anywhere that the membrane grows thin, either softened up by a high dose of DMT or hanging out on lonely highways. The latter possibility is of course far more interesting but how to demonstrate that's what's happening? Very tricky.

I take it you do believe the greys are real, and not only that but they are from Zeta Reticuli, and that they are working in some kind of collaboration with humans (government agencies?) to conduct human/alien genetic hybrid experiments? That's a lot to accept! At least in the absence of extraordinarily strong evidence, and I haven't seen it.

That said I'm not saying it can't be true; if psychedelics teach us anything, it's to always remember the limitations of our knowledge, and keep an open mind.

I know that Terence was always dismissive of the idea that Greys were here to conduct breeding experiments, and liked to crack jokes about "proctologists from Zeta Reticuli." As far as either Terence or me ever having personal abduction experiences, if they happened, the amnestic blocks have worked because I have no memory of anything like that happening. Terence certainly never related anything like that to me, except for that famous UFO described in *True Hallucinations,* which I believe he did see. I was there too but I was off in some other dimension, and I never saw it.

I have only two memories of possible anomalies that happened to me or Terence and unfortunately they are not very clear, nor very impressive. One happened to me in Hawaii when I was living in Manoa Valley. I was alone in my apartment, late at night, and I was reading something about UFOs or extraterrestrials—I forget what it was. Suddenly I got a strong message, like a telepathic command: go outside and look to the east. I did that. There was nothing there. Then as I continued to stare, I saw just the faintest sight of something that looked like a circular cloud, faintly glowing, not moving, and barely visible about 30 degrees above the horizon. It could have been a cloud; it looked like a cloud, and probably was one. If it was a UFO, it was pretty disappointing. I could barely see it. The only anomaly was the telepathic message to go look at the sky.

I don't remember Terence describing any UFO sighting that he or we had when we were kids. I do (vaguely, very vaguely!) remember something he related to me, in a conversation about DMT and the machine-like artifacts the "machine elves" sometimes show you. He said that he remembered my Dad loading us into the car one evening and driving us into the adobes outside of town. It was either to show us a UFO or to show us one of these artifacts, whatever it might have been. But even in Terence's description, it's not clear if he related this as a dream that he had about our father, or if he was recalling something that happened. Certainly I have no memory of this. And I don't think Terence thought of it as anything other than a dream, and I think that's what it was. It's that memory thing again! I mention this only in the interests of full disclosure. I do not believe that there was anything anomalous, I think it was Terence (an inveterate bullshitter and embellisher, remember) relating a dream that he may or may not have had.

RALPH: Thanks so much for your detailed response to my weird inquiry. You actually confirmed everything I thought I remembered of my conversations with Terence. And of course it's only speculation on my part, fed by reading in the extensive UFO and ET abduction literature. I have also been much influenced by my reading and conversations with John Mack, a very sober and perceptive scientist/psychiatrist, who won the case that Harvard filed against him accusing him of unscientific fabrication and inappropriate promulgation of evidence. The taboo in science against taking UFO/ET reports seriously is strong, much stronger than the taboo against taking psychedelic visions seriously. I think this must be because in the latter there is always the materialist excuse of "that's just a drug response." In the literature of UFO/ET encounters, that excuse is absent—once you accept the stories are being told by credible witnesses, even though your paradigm tells you they're "impossible."

I do remember Terence telling the story of a time your father took both of you out on a drive one night, inexplicably, and you spent quite a bit of time driving and then sitting in the car—with your father never explaining why he drove you all out there. Maybe it was your father who saw an UFO! Anyway—thanks again for your story fragments and puzzles.

DENNIS: Thanks for your confirmation of Terence's apocryphal story. So we either both had a false memory or this really happened. To the extent I remember this (and as I said it's so vague I can't even say it was not a dream) I remember T talking about it more than I remember the event, if it happened. But it's possible it did. It would be very uncharacteristic for our Dad to do something like this. As Terence related, and I seem to recall, this is how it came down: a lot of driving around out in the adobes—stopping, scanning the horizon, no explanation of what was going on. We certainly never saw a UFO or any kind of alien artifact. Did Dad even know what was going on? Doubtful. But this was just one of those things about Dad that showed to me anyway that he was more interested in "weird" phenomena than he ever let on, either to us or to his friends. To his friends, in the post-war shock of recovery from the personal and collective trauma of the war, he and they were all very invested in being part of the herd. Just "normal."

We used to get into big arguments about this when I was a teenager. He used to say something like, "the average guy just wants to live his life and have his routines, his friends, etc." And I would get furious about it. What made Dad cool in my teenage eyes (and I didn't think he was really very cool) but if he was, it was precisely because he was *not* "the average guy." And I used to point this out to him but he didn't want to hear it. He was very invested in thinking of himself that way. But he was a deeper thinker than most of his friends—he was interested in aviation, space travel, a regular reader of science fiction and *Fate* magazine, and he would bring these things home. So in some way, though Dad hated that T & I were weird and nerdy, he has to take some of the blame for that—or credit depending on how you see it. He was certainly not an "average guy." So who knows? Maybe Dad had an ET/UFO encounter at some point? I don't want to encourage unbridled speculation here but it's possible. Possible for anyone I suppose.

TWELVE

LESSONS FROM TORTOISE, WHALE, AND LIZARD

Three converging lines of influence have led me over time to an expanded worldview that recognizes the reality of nonmaterial beings, commonly called *spirits*. One was my participation in an Eastern-influenced meditation practice in which my clairvoyant perception of spirit beings and nonmaterial energy fields evolved naturally with practice. Another influence was my participation in wilderness vision quests facilitated by Steven Foster and Meredith Little of the School of Lost Borders in the Mojave Desert of Southern California. I appreciated the simple, down-to-earth way that Stephen and Meredith would speak of "calling in" the spirits of the desert and the plants and animals. A third line of influence was my connection with the anthropologist and educator Michael Harner and the practitioners associated with his Foundation for Shamanic Studies. He and his colleagues have expanded the existing social-science paradigm and confirmed the experiential reality of spirits as beings with whom one can intentionally connect with the shamanic drumming method of journeying.

In the past fifty years there has been, primarily in the Western world, a cultural and historical convergence of new research on psychoactive drugs with age-old indigenous traditions that use certain plants and fungi for religious and healing ceremonies. In my book *Green Psychology* (1999) I pointed out that the two main methods used cross-culturally for expanding states of consciousness are rhythmic drumming and vision-inducing plants or fungi. It appears that in the Northern Hemisphere regions of America, Europe, and Asia, the drumming method is more prevalent—the beat of the drum may be experienced as the hoofbeat of the shaman's vehicle animal. In the tropical and subtropical latitudes of the Americas and Asia, where there is a much greater diversity of plants and fungi, including those that affect states of consciousness, these are more likely to be used. Additionally, the greater humidity in the tropical latitudes makes the maintenance of a tight drum skin much harder—though various kinds of rattles, made of gourds with pebbles and the like, may be used to stimulate the sense of traveling and moving on land, on water, in the air, or under the earth.

The chanting or speaking of prayerlike invocations of spirits, especially animal spirits, as well as ancestral or deity spirits, is nearly universal among indigenous cultures, whether or not they use vision-inducing substances in their ceremonies. However, in contemporary groups experimenting with psychedelics or entheogens, prayers and spirit invocations are not necessarily widely used. The exceptions would be those who have adopted a ritual form from indigenous ceremonial teachers, or by those associated with one or another of the neo-pagan churches active in North America and Europe. This may be due to lingering discomfort that many Western people have with the open and explicit expression of spiritual concepts or beliefs. The secret question or reservation some people seem to hold is: *But I don't really believe in spirits—or do I?*

For myself, having grown up within the normal twentieth-century agnostic, materialist worldview, for whom experiencing a drug-induced altered state was at first considered a scientific experiment, the acceptance of the possible reality status of spirits developed gradually over a period of many years. I would emphasize, however, that my gradual acceptance of the possible autonomous reality of spirits remains anchored in the phenomenology of radical empiricism. In other words, I do not treat any and all visions of "beings" or "entities" as independently "real" until I have subjected them to the customary checks and balances of the empirical approach—which is essentially an ongoing, gradual, open-ended process. So, in a sense, the question whether I "believe in the existence of spirits," is as vacuous as the question of whether I believe in the existence of people would be.

In my workshops, I have integrated practices from the spiritual and shamanic traditions I learned through several different indigenous teachers. Most indigenous sacred ceremonies around the world involve invocations of the spirits of the four directions, the spirits specific to the local place, and the spirits of the time and season. (Some traditional ceremonies invoke six primary directions, counting also above and below.) The animal species and features metaphorically associated with the four directions vary according to local tradition and tribal lore, but the importance of recognizing and relating to the four cardinal directions is universal. I see them as relating us to the larger environment of planet Earth and beyond Earth to the whole solar system. North is north wherever you are on the Earth, even though magnetic north varies slightly over the precession cycle of thousands of years. Similarly, the sun always rises in the east and sets in the west, no matter what part of the planet you are on at the time.

In traditional ceremonies, these general invocations may then be followed, whether spoken aloud or not, by invocations and prayers to the animal spirits with whom one is personally connected; to plant and fungal spirits and those of the mineral world; to the members of our human family and ancestors, friends, and colleagues; to the greater culture-specific spirits, deities, and angels that we know from religious and spiritual traditions with which we are connected; and to planetary and cosmic deities. In the appendix to my book *Allies for Awakening* (2015), I give suggested poetic versions of such invocations that practitioners could use or adapt.

Variously called "power animals," "spirit animals," or "totemic animals," animal spirits have been the allies, guides, and teachers of shamanic practitioners since the most ancient hunter-gatherer and Stone Age times. We are speaking here of invoking, not so much a particular animal that we love, such as a pet dog or cat (although these could be included in an invocation), but rather the spirit or intelligence of a wild animal species—of Buffalo or Wolf, not this or that particular buffalo or wolf. The word *wild* is related to the word *will*. The wild creature is "self-willed" and sovereign, not subject to domestication or the will of another. In cultivating our connection and friendship with wild animal spirits we are reminded of our own wild and indigenous evolutionary heritage on planet Earth.

In the following three stories I will relate some experiences from dreams and visionary states that taught me some important lessons—in part painful ones—dealing with our human connection to the animal realm.

Desert Tortoise Encounter

In September 1991 I was conducting a vision-quest workshop for a group of about a dozen participants near the tiny Southern California desert town of Joshua Tree. We had rented the house of an artist for the weekend, which was situated near the boundary of the park. Most of the participants had done similar workshops with me before and were experienced travelers. The group included three or four psychiatrists, several psychologists, and a registered nurse.

We gathered on the Friday afternoon, some coming from the LA area, others, including me, from Northern California. Friday evening was devoted to bringing each other up to date on current life issues and intentions of vision and healing for the journeys to come. We were planning to make an excursion into the nearby desert state park during the daytime and use vision-assisting medicines on Saturday evening. The idea was first to connect with the spirits in the rocky desert around us, each person alone, and then to gather, after sharing stories, for the evening-group ceremony. First, explore the present outer natural environment, then explore the inner space.

I've always loved walking and climbing around in the mountainous

California desert environment. Though I grew up in European urban environments and prefer to live in the moderate clime of Northern California, I love the expansive horizon, the fierce dryness, and the brilliant light of the desert as a place for spiritual retreat and meditation. I sometimes think I may have had a past life as a desert hermit in the very early years of Christianity.

We walked off together from the parking area, climbing upward among giant boulders, until we found a gathering place from which we all took off alone in different directions, agreeing to return in about four hours. We were fasting, but everyone carried water. Some people took notebooks for writing or sketching. We told each other in which direction we were going, in case someone got injured—a standard vision-quest precautionary practice I had learned from Steven Foster. I walked off as well, delighting in the rich fragrance of desert plants and the alternation of blazing heat when in the sun and comforting warmth in the shade of the big rocks.

As we were starting to converge back to our agreed-upon meeting place, I came upon a magnificent specimen of the California desert tortoise (*Gopherus agassizii*) clambering slowly but surely among the giant rocks. His topmost shell was perhaps eighteen inches in diameter, all scratched and pockmarked from the impact of rocks and stones. I marveled at how this creature could move so sure-footedly, though very slowly, among the scattered boulders over the uneven terrain. Even more, I wondered where he could get enough water. (I somehow assumed it was a male, though did not know for sure.)

Taking advantage of his slow movement, I picked him up. Then I excitedly called the others to come over, and I picked him up again—to show, or rather to show off. Someone took a photo, which clearly shows my tense, contracted posture. Everyone was impressed and pleased at having encountered this magnificent creature. After I put him back down on the ground, we all started to clamber back down toward the house among the big rocks. All of a sudden I passed out and sank to the ground. I came to with a jolt of sharp pain in my foot, to find myself

Fig. 12.1. Ralph holding desert tortoise, notice the obviously cramped posture, 1991

Fig. 12.2. Bandaged foot, karmic consequence of Ralph's disrespect

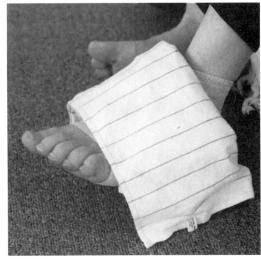

surrounded by concerned faces, some asking me, "How do you feel?" We joked later that while the psychiatrists were asking how I felt, the nurse knew to lower my upper body and raise my foot so blood could flow back to my head. It was apparent I had sprained my foot and passed out with the pain.

Supported by two strong pairs of shoulders, I slowly made it back to our house, and we proceeded to call around to local hospitals and clinics to see if we could find a doctor on call. It took a while, but we eventually did find an emergency room, where I was bandaged up and supplied with pain medication. We then proceeded with our long-delayed evening session, with me contemplating my bandaged foot. During that session, which went smoothly and peacefully, I got it: The fall and injury were karmic payback for my disrespect in picking up the tortoise. I did not seek permission from this magnificent creature to pick it up. If I had asked, I would surely have been refused—the slow-moving tortoise spends its entire life close to the earth and is incapacitated when carried. Dropping it from a height could be fatal. I had picked it up for my egotistical agenda of showing off.

I took some small comfort in the fact that I hadn't harmed the tortoise and that my disrespectful action was short-lived. During the session I connected to the king of that tortoise species and apologized sincerely and repeatedly. I want to be clear: In no way did I think that Tortoise was somehow punishing me for being disrespectful, somehow causing my injury. My injury was a natural accidental consequence of the arrogant inattentiveness involved in picking up the tortoise.

It took some weeks for me to heal the sprain and to regain full mobility, so I had ample opportunity to practice remorse in other journeys and meditations. The word *remorse* comes from the Latin *remordere*—"to bite again"—to extract the karmic lessons from one's action. I was learning my lesson. About one year later, I was on another California desert vision quest and saw a beautiful specimen of that tortoise. I saw him from about fifteen or twenty feet away and immediately stopped walking any closer. Of course he or she had already stopped

Fig. 12.3. California desert tortoise (*Gopherus agassizii*) photographed from a respectful distance, Yucca Valley, 1992

and was looking in my direction. I've confirmed many times what others have also noted: *animals in the wild always see us before we see them.* Our civilized existence is a contracted kind of consciousness.

I took the fact that Tortoise and I met as a sign that the karmic debt had been redeemed. We were allies again. Slowly I walked closer, murmuring expressions of greeting, respect, and admiration for the beautiful geometric patterns on its carapace—which it allowed me to photograph from a respectful distance.

———

Several months after the incident with the desert tortoise, I asked myself in a vision ceremony why some of the indigenous tribes of North America referred to their land as *Turtle Island.* After all, if you look at a two-dimensional map of the continent, there is nothing resembling a turtle or tortoise outline. It came to me that perhaps the Native Americans were seeing the Earth spherically in their clairvoyant visions, and seeing the continental land masses "floating" on the oceans. "Turtle islands" could be seen as an appropriate descriptive metaphor for all the continents: according to the accepted geological theory of plate tectonics, the continents are solid plates floating or swimming extremely slowly on the more liquid magma substrate of the lithosphere. So you could see how North and South America appear as the upper and lower plates of the giant Earth Turtle, as do the continental shelves of Eurasia, Africa, India, and Australia. The deeper perception encoded in the indigenous mythic symbolism had anticipated the findings of the modern scientific theory!

Whale Dreaming

During the 1980s I had became aware, like many others, of the groundbreaking research going on around the world on the extraordinary intelligence and sonic communication capabilities of whales and dolphins. I had met John Lilly in the late 1960s, and I knew of his work with LSD and with sensory isolation experiments, as well as of his pioneering research station, where dolphins were kept in a partly closed environment but had access to the open sea. At the Hollyhock retreat center near Vancouver, I met and became friends with Canadian journalist and ecologist Rex Weyler, who had written a book called *Song of the Whale*. In this book Rex described the extraordinary work and life of Dr. Paul Spong, a neuroscientist who had worked on the sensory capabilities of orcas in captivity. He found that they could learn sensory-discrimination skills very quickly and then would suddenly cease to "perform the task." These observations led him to conclude that the orcas were of superior intelligence and were communicating their despair and their contempt for their human captors. He recommended that the orcas should be freed from their "research imprisonment"— which promptly got him fired from his university job. He thereupon established an independent research station in the waters off Vancouver Island. Here the orcas could be observed moving freely through their natural environment while their sounds were being recorded—a project that continues to this day. Paul Spong and Rex Weyler were some of the original founders of the Greenpeace Save the Whales campaign.

I was fascinated to learn about the songs of whales and dolphins. In 1984 I attended a workshop with Paul Winter, the clarinetist who was first inspired by Roger Payne's famous 1970 recording of whale songs—*Song of the Humpback Whale*—and has since made several extraordinary recordings of human musicians playing with whales, wolves, dolphins, seals, and other creatures. In the workshop, Paul was enormously engaging as he encouraged each of us to choose an instrument and *just play*—playing music together like a free-flowing conversation between friends, "consorting," as he liked to call it. Part of the workshop, which was held in a retreat center on the Pacific Coast north of San Francisco, included a very intense sweat lodge run by a medicine man from the Tlingit people. I cried, sweated, and prayed for the whales, the dolphins, the orcas—and to open the hearts of the men who hunt them. A whale activist named Gigi Coyle spoke about an Australian legend of the Golden Dolphin, which was circulating around New Age circles at that time. As she spoke, she was channeling an orca spirit—or so it seemed to me from the even, lateral glances of her eyes.

In 1988 I had what some would call a "big dream" about whales. A big dream is one with such an emotional impact that you know right away that you won't forget it. In the dream, I was traveling with my wife and son in western England and Ireland. Four years before, we had actually been in Ireland for a conference of the International Transpersonal Association in Killarney. Touring around the country at that time, I felt enormously connected to the land, the people, and the culture—more so than I felt in Scotland, where my mother was born and where I lived as a child.

In the dream, we're in a small town with one church and one restaurant. I'm standing on top of a cliff looking out to sea. Then I notice that huge tidal waves are forming, and I'm warning the others that the waves might crash on the land and they should watch out. There is an ominous, deep, rumbling sound as well as crashing waves with high-flying spray. An enormous whale hurls himself out of the water and up the slope of rocky scree, actually flying overhead to land on top of the cliff, thrashing violently. I'm awestruck. I'm concerned that we might be hit by its thrashing tail and wonder how the magnificent creature is going to get back to the sea. But with another enormous push, it hurls and thrashes itself back down— swimming off into the ocean vastness.

Only two days later, as synchronicity would have it, I was scheduled to have a session with the well-known Swiss psychotherapist Dora Kalff, whose modality is Jungian sand-tray therapy—a process in which you place symbolic figurines in a tray with sand and a blue bottom, like water. When we met, I told her my whale dream and about the concerns that were distressing me at the time—the dishonesty, backstabbing, and manipulation that I perceived among some of the staff, faculty, and students at the California Institute for Integral Studies (CIIS), the graduate school where I had been an administrator and teacher for nearly twenty years already. I noticed my strong emotional charge as I was telling Dora Kalff about this situation, which was obviously stressful for me.

Dora said, "The whale is thrashing around on land, not in his natural watery element, but then returns to it. The Self can do this, as you are doing, and doesn't need help from the ego. The whale finding its way back to the sea symbolizes your Self finding its way back to its natural home—despite all the rough terrain on the way." In the sand-tray, I had created an island in the shape of a whale, with a circular opening in the middle. Dora suggested that the whale island is the center of being, with an open eye of self-awareness. I was enormously relieved by her interpretation of my dream and the sand-tray. In considering my spiritual and ecological concerns, I thought the whale coming onto the land also suggested a kind of reaching out from the cetacean species to the human species—to make alliances, to work together to confront the desperation of our situation.

In September 1991 I attended a three-day gathering of the North American Bioregional Association, held at the Enchanted Hills Camp in Napa, California. One of the presenters was a whale ecologist and activist called John McLean. He guided an imagery meditation in which we were to find a way to communicate with whales. In the session I went through a door and then found myself in a cave, at the shore, communicating telepathically with a whale and expressing the wish for us to be friends. The response from Whale was immediate, saying, "We're friends already, have been for a long time." I was struck by something John McLean had been saying about whales being at home in the sea the way we upright walking primates are at home on the land. But in my mind's eye I had been seeing the whale's power and ease in the sea, and comparing it to my seeming powerlessness and insecurity. Our frail, skinny, two-legged human form, compared to the massive strength of the whale form. Then Whale said to me, telepathically: "You can be on the land the way we are in the sea." Then I began to feel strength and ease within my own body. I realized that scale or size is relative. What is important is the attitude of self-acceptance and ease with your body, as it is, whether massive or skinny.

My next encounter with the Whale Spirit occurred in 1996, when I turned sixty. With some friends we were experimenting with the seeds of a little-known South American shamanic vision plant whose scientific name is *Anadenanthera colubrina*. The seeds of this plant, which contain bufotenine, are ground up and can be snuffed or smoked when sprinkled on some other leaves. My friends and I used both methods. I mention these details of ingestion only to emphasize that the connections to Spirit and spirit animals are independent of the particular kind of altered state one is in. I did have some discomfort, a burning or stinging sense in my nasal passages after the snuff. I asked Spirit for help with that, though I wasn't explicitly thinking of whales.

The next thing I notice is that I seem to be under water, the whole space is under water, and the room we are in is now a large aquarium. The burning sensation is gone. I seem to be able to breathe underwater with no problem. Various brightly colored creatures and objects are floating and weaving around. The bed I have been lying on starts moving out to sea, like a raft on a river. Now it is transformed into the back of a whale, a bit larger than me—an orca. I ask-think, "Where are we going?" The reply from my orca vehicle comes: "You can request where you want to go." I say-think, "Will you take me to see your family?" I realize we both can move underwater without a problem. I'm not seeing the orca that's carrying me, but I feel her body like a submarine raft. I somehow know it's a female. I can see and sense other whales and various fish passing overhead. Then I do meet her family. There is a wonderful feeling of well-being and mutual acceptance. I ask for help in healing a long-standing pain in my groin. Suddenly I am out of the water and see a tiny dollhouse, in which I'm trying to rearrange the furniture. At first I think it might relate to a childhood memory, but I don't get any other associated memories. Instead, the healing message from the Whale Teacher was, "Don't bother to rearrange the furniture in your childhood memories—it's all long past. You don't need to do anything. Just let it be."

I nonverbally expressed my deep gratitude to the magnificent Whale Being, who had visited me several times over the years—in a dream, in a meditative state, in a plant-substance-induced state. Our teaching-healing connection was not state-dependent—it was essential, authentic, and continuing, a true friendship across dimensions of reality. One more example occurred in a dream about fifteen years later.

I'm learning how to send and receive sounds to communicate with whale-like beings. These whale beings live permanently underwater and have a kind of consciousness very different from the human. I'm being shown or told that the key to communication with them, as with anyone, is to clearly state and declare, verbally and telepathically, your intention in the encounter. Stating your own intention and recognizing the intention of the other was and is a matter of interspecies and interdimensional etiquette more basic and important than stating your name, which could come afterward.

I reflected on how this principle contrasts with the accepted social etiquette among humans, who, when being introduced to one another, state their name first and then discuss their agenda for the meeting. At least that is the ideal, which is not always practiced in situations with hidden agendas. I was glad to receive the basic lesson in interspecies etiquette, in which the clarity and integrity of intention is paramount.

Lizard—Time Traveler and Trickster

In 1986 I turned fifty and went on my first vision quest in the Mojave Desert in California, having been expertly prepared by Steven Foster and Meredith Little of the School of Lost Borders. I made my campsite among gigantic rocks on a stony ridge and spent my days walking slowly along the ridge or down into the canyon, taking care to find resting places that provided shade during the maximum midday heat as well as protection from the roaring desert winds. I would sing softly as I walked, offering prayers to the elements and the spirits of plants and animals. I walked down into the canyon, recapitulating and reviewing every year of my life in my mind's eye, arriving in the canyon floor as an infant and then climbing back up through the years, burning off toxic memory images of shame, guilt, and pain along the way. I was ecstatic. At night I set up my sleeping bag in a protected sandy spot and drifted off gazing at the glittering stars and constellations.

There were lizards galore in this place, gorgeously hued in electric blues and emerald greens, flashing and flitting around and then sitting perfectly still. On my walks I kept seeing them, talking to them admiringly, trying to photograph them—without much success, as they would flit off when I looked away momentarily. I tried to estimate if there was a safe distance at which they would let me approach. I would take one step and then stop—I could see them tilt their head with one eye in my

Figure 12.4. Lizard, possibly a whiptail, basking on a rock in Yucca Valley, 1991

direction, and I would softly murmur my appreciation and admiration, asking for permission to come closer.

I thought about their movement pattern—flitting very fast and then stopping totally still—and I wondered about its function. A desert ecologist I talked to confirmed that this is a camouflage pattern: when the lizards are still, the patterns on their backs blend in with the rocks and the grasses, and roaming predators like coyotes don't see them. And I couldn't see them either! A couple of times I was watching one of the lizards from about ten feet away under some bushes. We were making eye contact, and I took very slow steps to come closer and squat down for a better look—and when I did, he was gone. I never saw him leave, although I was focused on the place he had occupied. It was as if he had left an image of himself for me to see—but he took off and left the "costume" in place. I was impressed, to say the least. This was lizard magic!

I was wondering about the ecological function of the strange push-up movements that lizards make, whereby they push themselves up high on their front legs, while the long tail stays on the ground. Most of the guidebooks I've read are evasive about this maneuver, if they mention it at all, or they say it's a mating signal—a male is trying to show off to attract a female. But this seemed absurd to me. Many times I've seen a lizard sitting alone on a high rock, doing these push-ups, when there aren't any others nearby to see this performance. But when I practiced empathic merging with the lizard sitting on the high rock, putting myself in its place, I got it: they elevate themselves to get a better view. If I lived most of my existence with my body touching the ground, I would also welcome the opportunity to get a better view of what's around and what's up ahead.

In 1987, about a year after my first meeting with the Lizard Spirit, there was a gathering of friends at the house Terence and Kathleen McKenna were living in at that time, on the Big Island of Hawaii. Leo Zeff was also present, along with Tom Pinkson, George and Requa Greer, and several other friends. The purpose of the weeklong gathering was to compare notes on various kinds of entheogenic substances and strategize about ways such substances could be most usefully integrated into society. Although there was no formal structure, Leo Zeff was the informal elder guide because of his age and his experience as a psychedelic psychotherapist. Terence and Kat talked about their experiences cultivating and growing various entheogenic plants and fungi. Tom Pinkson, George Greer, and I talked about possible therapeutic applications and uses of these substances. Of course there were some experiential journeys.

We arranged ourselves, sitting or lying, in an approximate circle during these ceremonies. As usual for me, I would alternate between looking at inner visions with my eyes closed and looking at the space above me. Soon after we started I suddenly "saw" that a giant iguana had landed on the roof. I recognized him from the massive tail and the squat head. I felt no fear—on the contrary, I felt he was our protector. My lizard encounters in the California desert were fresh in my mind.

I had also been reading about the Mayan creator deity Itzamná, with whom I felt very connected. Itzamná was a sky god, considered a creator deity and the inventor of writing and divination. Some Mayan vase paintings show him as a man with a hooked nose, holding a writing tablet, with a lizard on his head. I felt drawn to and related to this mythic figure, so I was glad to see him in his lizard form as our protector and vision maker. Tuning in with this lizard form also had healing effects on some tensions I was holding in my back and spine.

As the evening progressed, I was intermittently looking up at the ceiling, at the pattern made by the dark roof beams and the lighter segments of the skylights. An image coalesced of a man sitting on the ground at the entrance to a cave and looking out at the lighter open area outside. I couldn't make out any details of his face—I seemed to be seeing him from some distance—but he was wearing a wide-brimmed hat and holding a staff while looking out at the lighter open area. Every now and again during the next couple of hours, after other visions and conversations in our group, I would return to this vision on the ceiling, and it was still there. I did not know what to make of it or how it related to me—or even if it related to me at all.

It wasn't until several months later, in the summer of 1988, that I finally recognized this vision as an actual foreseeing of the future. I was on another vision-quest journey with the School of Lost Borders in the desert canyons of California's Inyo Mountains. I had found a sort of cave entrance made by a large overhanging rock and decided it would be my resting place. I was sitting by the entrance of this cave, with the darkness behind me and the sunlit valley area in front. I was wearing my wide-brimmed hat, and my staff was nearby. Then I got it—*I was the man in the vision seen six months before*, in a kind of precognitive preview.

In reflecting on this experience, it became clear to me that when you have a vision of some kind, you can never really know exactly whether the vision is of an actual experience you will have in the future—in other words a precognitive or prophetic vision. There is nothing in the vision itself, no little extra label, that tells you, "this is actually going to happen or might actually be your experience." What exactly will happen "remains to be seen." A vision is not a prediction based on probability estimates, like a weather forecast or a stock-market quote. It points to a possibility and is open-ended as to how it may relate to your personal life experience.

There are traditions of visionary prophets and seers, the oracles of ancient times or the psychics of modern times, who are able to, or claim to be able to, tune in to someone else's future experience, either using their own intuition or some divination system like astrology or the Tarot. These methods imply that there is someone who asks, someone who consults the oracle or the psychic, with a question. The vision I had with the medicine in Hawaii was not like that. It was a gratuitous gift from Spirit—unrequested and unrecognized until half a year later.

In 2001, fourteen years after the vision in Hawaii, I had another encounter with the Lizard Being, in real time-space, in Northern California, where I live. I was walking in the park on a warm spring day. There were many insects buzzing and humming around. Two butter-flies, one blue and one yellow, were doing a courtship dance in the air in front of me. It was a dizzying performance, as I watched them soar and tumble around each other. I reflected on the teaching I seemed to be getting—that two very different beings, of different coloring, can be in a love relationship. Later I saw what appeared to be a small young snake sliding through the grass by the side of the path. I had a momen-tary impulse to bend down and pick her up, but then I remembered the lesson of Grandfather Tortoise, and let her be with a blessing of good-will. That gesture of letting be, of not interfering, seemed to trigger a sequence of remarkable events.

Shortly thereafter, as I continued walking along a narrow, hilly path, I saw a lizard a yard or two in front of me on the path. I immediately stopped and squatted down to commune with him, and as I did, so I saw him dart straight toward my feet and run up one of the legs of my pants. I was so startled by this unexpected maneuver that I stood up, stepped back, and shook out my pants legs. Then I didn't see him anymore and assumed he had disappeared into the tall grasses. I did have the thought, for no rational reason, that he ran toward me because he felt I was safe for him, because he'd seen me not pick up the snake. I proceeded with my walk for another twenty minutes or so back to my car. I drove back to my home, which took about fifteen minutes, then to the post office and talked to the postmaster (another ten minutes) and then drove to the local hardware store to get something for the garden (another twenty minutes). As I was pulling into the parking lot at Friedman Brothers, I felt some kind of movement on my left shoulder. I reached back with one hand and realized the lizard was underneath my outer shirt on my shoulder. He'd traveled with me all the way from the park almost an hour before!

I was amazed. I got out of the car and very carefully took off my outer shirt. There he was, inside the shirtsleeve. I didn't want to let him down or shake him out onto the hot asphalt of the parking lot. So I carefully put the shirt, with the lizard still hiding in it, on to the car seat, and he promptly disappeared under the seat. I wanted to make sure he would be in a safe natural environment, so after I got my purchases, I drove to another area, with lots of grass and bushes. I tried in vain to coax the lizard to come out—he was clearly hiding from me and other humans. I left all the car doors open and walked away for about ten minutes. After I returned, he was finally gone.

So here was Lizard the Trickster, first giving me lessons in sudden, unexpected movement and in trust and concealment. But then, as so often in North American native stories, the Trickster himself gets tricked and ends up going for an unexpected ride. I was very happy that he didn't come to any harm when he was with me. Our friendship is secure, and I know our next encounter will also be surprising—but interesting!

THIRTEEN

DREAM TEACHINGS WITH G. I. GURDJIEFF

In our memoir *Birth of a Psychedelic Culture* (2010), Ram Dass and I, with Gary Bravo, wrote about how our group of psychedelic researchers had become aware of the Gurdjieff and Ouspensky lineage of teachings when we were searching for philosophical precursors for our explorations in consciousness. Tim Leary and I, with Alpert providing backup support, had been adapting *The Tibetan Book of the Dead* as a guidebook for psychedelic inner journeys, sheared of the specifics of Tibetan Buddhist iconography. This book was first published in 1964 as *The Psychedelic Experience—A Manual Based on the Tibetan Book of the Dead*. It became something of a best seller in the underground psychedelic culture and was translated into numerous languages. It is still in press in a variety of editions, including an audio recording.

In the fall of 1963, a small group of about a dozen people, including Leary, Alpert, and me, moved into a mansion on the Millbrook estate in upstate New York, which became our home for the next half-dozen years and the place where we continued our explorations. Besides finding guidance in Tibetan Buddhism, we also found literary inspiration in the later works of the Nobel Prize–winning German novelist Hermann Hesse (1877–1962). Leary and I wrote an essay for *The Psychedelic Review,* our quarterly journal, suggesting that several of Hesse's novels, especially *Journey to the East* and *Steppenwolf,* contained disguised metaphorical descriptions of psychedelic experiences—a suggestion strenuously denied by the Hesse family heirs. Hesse, who lived in Switzerland, was a pacifist who had been attacked by the Nazis and whose writings were hardly known in the United States. His novels went through a dramatic upswing in popularity in the 1960s, with the rise of the international counterculture, and possibly stimulated also by our endorsement.

Searching for guidance and inspiration for our work, which had moved from psychology into the borderlands of spirituality and Eastern philosophy, we started to read the writings of P. D. Ouspensky (1878–1947) and G. I. Gurdjieff (1866–1949), who was Ouspensky's teacher. I remember how excited I was to discover a whole vast system of ideas in which processes and practices of consciousness expansion, or "becoming conscious," as it was called, were the central concern. We imagined and began to speculate about finding information about the use of consciousness-expanding drugs in such sources. We also wanted to experiment with nondrug methods of heightening consciousness in a search for some kind of common ground.

Fig. 13.1. G. I. Gurdjieff.
Photo from Ralph Metzner's
personal collection

In the early days of our Millbrook community, we experimented with a variant of Gurdjieff's "stop" exercise. At unpredictable intervals during the day, a bell would ring, and then you were supposed to stop whatever you were doing for two minutes and just observe what you were doing, becoming aware of your physical, emotional, and mental state. It was exquisitely difficult to do, very frustrating as well as enlightening—about our lack of awareness. Then we heard about a teacher of what was called the "Gurdjieff work" in New York, Willem Nyland (1890–1975). We had probably heard of Nyland through Felix Morrow, who was the publisher of *The Psychedelic Experience* and who was also a student of the Gurdjieff work. We invited Mr. Nyland to come up to Millbrook for a discussion about Gurdjieff's teachings and consciousness expansion. This was in the mid-1960s, so Nyland had evidently heard from the sensationalist media about our work with what we were calling "consciousness-expanding" psychedelic drugs—and was predisposed to disapprove.

We were told that Nyland wouldn't come to the somewhat dilapidated seventy-five-year-old Big House, the mansion where our motley community of seekers lived, but he did agree to meet with some of us at the Bungalow, a more modern spread where the Hitchcock brothers, owners of the estate, lived when they were in residence. The meeting did not go well. Tim Leary asked Nyland whether Gurdjieff ever wrote or said anything about drugs affecting consciousness. Nyland refused to consider the possibility that Gurdjieff might have known about or used some unknown psychedelic substance. When I asked him about a passage in Ouspensky where Gurdjieff is quoted as saying that there is a "Fourth Way," the way of "the sly man," who takes a pill that allows him to go beyond personality and become aware of essence, Nyland dismissed the idea, saying, "No, no, Ouspensky didn't know anything."

Then Leary asked him, "Don't you think Gurdjieff would have improvised? His entire life looks like a series of improvisations to changing conditions and experimentation with various methods of teaching." Nyland said, "I have been teaching the work exactly the way Gurdjieff taught it, for the past twenty years." He seemed to take it as a point of pride that his words and methods, expounding the master's teachings, hadn't changed and were exactly the same years later. We thought it was kind of rigid and judgmental. But he then proceeded to give a comprehensive, lucid, condensed outline of the Gurdjieffian system that was very beautiful.

Some of us started going down to New York City to attend Nyland's weekly meetings. On our trips down the Tacoma Parkway, a two-hour car ride, one of us would read aloud from Gurdjieff's book *All and Everything: Beelzebub's Tales to His Grandson* to the others. About a year later, Leary, Alpert and I had a private meeting with Nyland. He had been scolding me on the phone about Tim's behavior. Was he conscientious, was he responsible or wasn't he just a publicity seeker? Undeniably there was considerable truth in his criticism. During the meeting he lectured us sternly. He said whatever the drugs did, "they could not give you an *I* or help you develop one, and this was the real task." I think the three of us lost interest in Mr. Nyland after that, although my wife, Susan Homer, continued to study with him for several more years. None of us lost our interest and high regard for Gurdjieff himself or for his work and his writings.

— —

After our small group of consciousness explorers had been living in the Millbrook community for about a year, an opportunity arose for me to accompany a sort of pilgrimage to India in a group led by Gayatri Devi. Mataji, as she was called, was an Indian spiritual teacher in the lineage of Ramakrishna and Vivekananda. She had founded ashrams in Los Angeles and Boston, had tried LSD once, and was supportive of our exploration of its spiritual potentials. Although I was not one of her formal devotees, I loved and admired Mataji and jumped at the opportunity to go on this month-long pilgrimage to various ashrams and temple sites in India in her company. I respected the *bhakti* devotional tradition and participated in their chanting and prayer ceremonies, although

I recognized that my path was clearly more the path of knowledge and yogic practices—what Gurdjieff and Ouspensky were calling the Fourth Way. I took a copy of *All and Everything* with me on the trip to India, and every morning, with the traditional Indian cup of chai, I would read from this amazingly complex and difficult tome, trying to decipher its abstruse teachings.

In the decades to follow, my interest in Gurdjieff's teachings continued and grew. I was totally fascinated by his second book, *Meetings with Remarkable Men,* in which he relates stories of his travels in Central Asia seeking fragments of "forgotten knowledge" from various teachers he met. I also read many books by his various followers and students. A. R. Orage and J. G. Bennett were the ones I resonated with the most, besides Ouspensky. But I never felt a need to become a disciple in any of the various communities or lineages of Gurdjieff "work," as it is called.

Tim Leary and I, along with others who studied the Gurdjieff-Ouspensky work, soon recognized that it was pointless to try to somehow fit psychedelics into that framework of consciousness practice. The seekers and explorers in that lineage did not have the awareness-amplifying substances to work with, or if they did, had them only to a very limited extent. For Gurdjieff and his disciples, the main practice consists of "work on oneself" or "self-remembering," as it was also called, while doing physical labor on assigned tasks. An additional practice in some groups consisted of movement exercises and dances derived from Sufi traditions—also performed with conscious intention and concentration. But both Leary and I soon let go of our naive attempts to somehow legitimize or support the use of psychedelics through possible references in other lineages of esoteric spiritual teachings.

When I became involved with the School of Actualism during the 1970s, I discontinued the use of psychedelic substances to focus attention on learning that school's carefully programmed series of *agni yoga* meditation practices. I wrote about these in my book *Maps of Consciousness,* which was published in 1971. Like many Western seekers of Eastern wisdom who had mind-opening experiences with psychedelics, I realized that the substances, carefully used, could amplify the perception of subtle changes of consciousness, but their use needed to be integrated with, or, better yet, preceded by practice in concentration.

During the late 1970s and 1980s I did not read or think much about Gurdjieff and his teachings, although in my study of the light-fire energy methods and in the literature of the European alchemists, I found many resonant connections with his teachings of self-observation. I realized also that the practice of self-observation and self-remembering—basically mindfulness—was a mutually reinforcing accompaniment to the light-fire yogic meditations. During the mid- to late 1980s, I began to go through an extremely painful separation from the School of Actualism, as well as the teachers and my fellow students in that group, which had increasingly become a cult.

In meetings of the upper-level students and teaching staff I was accused of unconsciously being a "dark force channel." I was made the designated scapegoat, who because of my supposedly deviant entanglements was somehow mysteriously responsible for the bad things happening in the organization, including the leaders' own obvious blunders and psychological naïveté. Finally I was removed from the teaching staff, other students were told to stay away from me, and I was told I needed special intensive "x-outs" to remove the dark force residues. Rather than submitting to this supposed "rehabilitation," I resigned. I had to deal with the painful effects of this unrelenting barrage of negativity and the complete psychic severance from the people who had been my closest companions and trusted teachers for many years. I learned to do so by inner questioning and trying to understand the truth behind the hurtful condemnations.

During those two decades of first involvement with and then disengagement from the Actualism group, my understandings of the workings of an esoteric school were very much informed by what I had read in Gurdjieff's and Ouspensky's writings. Like some Zen and Sufi teachers, Gurdjieff in particular often seemed to be saying that you have to experience (or deliberately induce) a wrenching disconnection from your external guru or teacher—in order to connect to your own inner essence Spirit source. There's a Zen saying, for example, that "you have to walk on the teacher's head in order to become enlightened." Such sayings were seemingly designed to counteract the idealizing tendency, the tendency to put the guru in some kind of an exalted, superhuman position as someone who could do no wrong and could not be mistaken—a tendency that provides obvious power temptations for the guru or teacher.

In any event, I practiced relating to these events in that way. I also practiced refraining from resentment against the teachers, who were rejecting me for spurious reasons having to do with their own personal inclinations. I was greatly assisted in this process through the support of my close friend Angeles Arrien, who was a high-level initiate in the secret teachings of her native Basque culture. In fact, she related that she was an emissary from her Basque teachers, who were interested in some kind of collaborative project with our meditation school. As it turned out, the Actualism teachers were too fixated on the superiority of their own way for any collaboration to get off the ground. In fact they seemed to feel somehow threatened by the contact with the Old World Basque teachings. My personal connection with Angeles Arrien provided me with salutary corrective perspectives for the distortions and weird accusations to which I was subjected.

In retrospect, it seems that a complete separation from the school, and from its founders and teachers, was necessary. I also remember being shocked at the fact that it took me about two to three years before I was able to reestablish my former network of friends and professional colleagues, from whom I had inadvertently become separated as a result of my involvement in the cult. I should add, however, that I never stopped practicing the light-fire yoga methods I learned from those teachers. I consider the techniques among the greatest gifts I have received in my life. I continue to incorporate and develop them further in my teaching and psychotherapy practice, including my work with awareness-amplifying entheogenic substances.

It was not until the 1990s, about ten years after the painful break with the Actualism school, that I started receiving teachings from Gurdjieff in the dream state—coming back, as it were, to a teacher I had connected with many years before.

In 1991 I had my first dream that involved Gurdjieff.

I'm in a group that is getting practice instructions from G., who then proceeds to take a phone call. People in the group start wandering off to cross a nearby river. When we return to the meeting place, G. is furiously berating everyone for not having waited for his instructions.

This was a classic Gurdjieffian Sufi tale. Teachers in those traditions may express anger toward their disciples and students, seemingly unjustly, in order to separate them from their idealizing identifications. Gurdjieff was notorious for alienating, sometimes with apparent emotional brutality, his closest followers, including Ouspensky. This was in marked contrast with Russell Schofield, founder of the School of Actualism, who was primarily a hands-on bodywork healer and who was soft-spoken and quiet to the point of inscrutability. After years of confusing exposure to deception and intrigue, I found the direct, if brutal, approach of Gurdjieff, as it was related, refreshing.

Then, about a month later in 1991, I had a series of dreams involving Gurdjieff that were among the most astonishing of my life.

I'm with Gurdjieff while we're traveling in the Caucasus Mountains. He tells me that one of his students or associates saved the lives of several others, but did it by revealing some esoteric secrets he had sworn to keep. As a result he had to die for violating his oath. I realize I was that person, and reexperience the dying process. I feel very close to G., like a personal friend. We're walking, talking, and joking around. He tells me that the story of this friend of his is related in his book Meetings with Remarkable Men.

The dream seemed to suggest that in a previous incarnation of mine I actually knew Gurdjieff personally during the 1880s and 1890s when, as a young man, he was traveling in Central Asia with a group he called "Seekers of Truth," visiting remote monasteries and esoteric schools. I had found these tales extraordinarily interesting and engaging when I first read them in the 1960s. But it had never occurred to me even remotely that "I" might have been involved in them in another life. I started to comb through *Meetings with Remarkable Men* to see if I could identify the person to whom he was referring. The results of this research, which I have carried out intermittently several times in the past twenty years, were ambiguous, but in part also tantalizingly suggestive.

Gurdjieff wrote about a younger Russian man he met in his travels called Soloviev, a penniless alcoholic with a terrible past history. Gurdjieff wrote that he had managed to cure Soloviev of his alcoholism using hypnosis—implanting in his subconscious mind such an aversion to alcohol that even the sight of a bottle made him sick. "Soloviev, who became my friend and comrade, also later was an authority on what is called Eastern medicine in general, and on Tibetan medicine in particular, and he was also the world's greatest specialist in the knowledge of the action of opium and hashish on the psyche and organism of man" (Gurdjieff 1963, 134). Though I have no particular knowledge of Tibetan medicine in this life, the effects of drugs on the psyche have been a central interest of mine, about which I have written several books. So here is one possible confirmation.

Gurdjieff related that Soloviev became a member of the expedition that traveled to visit a hidden monastery of the Sarmoung brotherhood. To reach it, they had to travel for several days with their eyes blindfolded and swear an oath never to reveal its location. When the expedition later crossed the Gobi desert, there is mention of some secrets of the desert kept by local inhabitants. "Soloviev joined the group of persons I have already mentioned, the Seekers of Truth. . . . He became a full member of this group and from then on, thanks to his persistent and conscientious efforts, he not only worked for the attainment of his individual perfection but at the same time took a serious part in all our general activities and expeditions. . . . During one of these expeditions, in the year 1898, he died from the bite of a wild camel in the Gobi Desert" (Gurdjieff 1963, 164–5).

While they were camping out in the desert, the group encountered a herd of wild camels. Soloviev, a "passionate hunter," seized his rifle and ran after them. When he did not return after a couple of hours, the group went searching for him and eventually found his dead body in the sand, with his "neck bitten half through." Gurdjieff wrote that they made a litter and carried Soloviev's body back to the camp. "All of us were overwhelmed with heart-rending grief, for we had all loved this exceptionally good man." After burying the body in the desert "with great solemnity in the heart of the desert, we immediately left that for us accursed place" (Gurdjieff 1963, 175–6).

In a curiously confirming detail, in the year 2000 I had two dream fragments on successive nights, where I sensed an enormous camel's head right next to my head, in one of which the camel is licking it. The extensive literature on reincarnation and past-life memories provides considerable anecdotal evidence that the fragmentary perception-memory of a sudden violent death may be carried over into a future life—until the trauma is recognized and thereby healed.

The long 1991 dream involving Gurdjieff also included several other teaching episodes. In these dream memories, I was just there with him and have no way of knowing whether I was there as Soloviev or as my twentieth-century self.

I go with G. to a restaurant where an elderly woman, who is interested in him, asks if he can cook, because she wants to marry him. I say jokingly, "Oh, no, he can't cook." He winks at me and proceeds to give a demonstration of magic. He leaves a small covered dish on the table and walks out. The dish is a shapeless mass that turns into a steak. As we continue to look at it, the meat turns into a miniature calf, lying on the table. He has somehow reversed the cooking process. I say to the people in the restaurant, who are blown away, that they'll never be able to tell anyone this story, because their friends won't believe them. I'm very animated. Everyone leaves the restaurant.

I go to a room where G. is sitting, and I ask his help for a woman friend who has just been assaulted and robbed. His face starts to change dramatically. A piece of his head breaks off and flies outside, where it turns into a large mechanical bird, which flies off to search for the robber.

In a further dream that same night,

I meet with G. again. He asks me for advice on how to raise money, which astounds me.

I had read his essay "The Material Question," appended to *Meetings with Remarkable Men,* in which he relates the many unusual and ingenious ways, some of them borderline unethical, which he used to raise money for his travels and research. In contrast, I felt I was always struggling to find ways to support my research, teaching, and writing, which tended to cross accepted academic and professional boundaries because of my research with mind-expanding drugs. In the dream,

after I get over my astonishment, I suggest he lead travel tours to Mongolia. We pore over some maps of Mongolia together.

This dream did relate to my present life—I have traveled and conducted workshops in the United States, South America, and several Western and Eastern European countries. At one point I was seriously considering and planning some workshops in India and the Far East.

During the next ten or twelve years, it seems I had a dream involving Gurdjieff about every couple of years. In one of these,

I am at first looking at photos of him and his companions walking through the cold Caucasus Mountain territory. Then I actually see them, bathing naked in the icy rivers to strengthen themselves.

Bathing in icy rivers is a practice that was described in one of his student's accounts. A couple of years later, I saw him in another dream, seemingly late in life and looking much older, coming and going among his disciples. (Of course, this chronological sequence of my dream meetings with G., has no linear relationship to the chronology of his actual physical life, since he died in 1949).

In 1997 I had another dream meeting with Gurdjieff that had all the features of a real encounter.

In appearance he is physically short but very powerfully built. As I meet him, a tremendous upwelling of love is evoked in me. There is a sense of churning waves of love energy in my heart center, incoming and outflowing, so intense that I wake up. Simultaneously, I realize that he deliberately evoked that feeling in me, so that I would become lucid in the dream. It was as if he had reached into my chest with his hands and moved my heart.

In 2005 I had the first of a series of dreams with Gurdjieff that involved my use of consciousness-amplifying medicines and the training programs I had developed in what I was calling Alchemical Divination. I had been teaching people how the divination methods can be used both with and without entheogenic amplification. One of the substances we had been using was 5-methoxy-DMT, which we had code-named *Jaguar*. Its use and effects are described in my book *The Toad and the Jaguar* (2013). In the dream,

I'm with Gurdjieff and a group of students on a boat. We're studying and discussing the use of the Jaguar medicine. He asks me to give him my entire stash, which piques me. Then he asks me: How are we going to treat all

these people? We make a tea for each of twelve people, apparently of twelve different types—so everyone gets a taste. G. looks at everyone in turn, testing them. He looks at me with his huge eyes—probing but kind. I marvel at how he always has such a deep impact on me.

Thinking about my piqued reactions to his demand that I give him my entire supply, I realized later that this was another example of his teaching. He was not interested in getting my stash—after all this was the dream world—but in making me aware of the holding pattern in my dynamic. It was like the story Ram Dass tells about his teacher, Neem Karoli Baba, demanding that he hand over all his LSD: the guru knew it would activate his pride and vanity.

In 2006 I had a dream in which Gurdjieff taught me a significant extension of one of the Alchemical Divination processes I had developed and was currently teaching in my groups. This process, which I call the Medicine Wheel of the Life Cycle, involves reviewing the main stages of the life cycle: first, the formative years of childhood, adolescence, and early adulthood; next, the middle years of the thirties, forties, and fifties, of family life and work in the community, from the perspective of our feminine and masculine identities; and fourth, the old age and elder years of the sixties and beyond. In this divination arranged as a medicine wheel with four points of the compass, we review and reconnect with key events, persons, and lessons from the past and preview the future stages, with anticipation of our inevitable death. This process corresponds to the usual linear way of conceiving one's life story in medicine, psychology, and education—from birth to death.

In our circle rituals, we would tune in to each quadrant of the Medicine Wheel with guided and amplified divination. The process always involved a double movement of attention and awareness: first, tuning in to your self-image at that stage of your life, and second, integrating those past perceptions into your present self-concept—how you have become the person you presently are (Metzner 2017, 175–86).

In the dream Gurdjieff is showing me further possibilities of my divination work with the Medicine Wheel of the Life Cycle. He gives me a long, complex name (which I couldn't bring back from the dream) for each of the four quadrants. In the dream, G. is suggesting that after exploring each phase individually in the usual clockwise direction, from the formative times of childhood and youth to the time of old age and death, we could spin the wheel in the opposite direction, counterclockwise, starting with the end of life. He communicates to me that with this way of working with the Life Cycle Medicine Wheel, we would see the four personas or masks for each stage being taken off or released, as it were, and the soul essence revealed.

From this dream teaching, I took Gurdjieff to be suggesting a second process with the Life Cycle Medicine Wheel, starting with the life-review at the end of life. Although there is always great uncertainty and anxiety about the timing and manner of our demise, we do have absolutely certain knowledge of the inevitability of our death. The process would therefore start by tuning in to the end of life, and from there rolling the personal clock of time and memory backward to conduct a kind of life review of old age, masculine and feminine adult personas, and lastly childhood and birth.

In the Alchemical Divination groups, we practiced working with the life cycle in this counterclockwise direction as well as in the normal way from birth to death. The results were dramatic: by starting with the naturally anticipated end-of-life phase, a certain liberating detachment was experienced, as well as a greater freedom to delve into difficult aspects of our remembered life experience. It seemed this was *the soul's perspective—that essence within us that precedes our conception and birth and continues beyond our personal ending.*

It was in the context of this dual practice I came to a new understanding of the two key mottos that run through much of the alchemical literature of the European Middle Ages. One of these is *natura naturans*—"nature doing everything naturally." This is also the fundamental concept in traditional Chinese and Indian medicine, as well as in western Hippocratic and indigenous medicinal practice: that the body basically heals itself, and we just need to support that process. We can rely on our primal, unconditioned, instinctual mind to sustain our health and well-being as we go through the life cycle from conception to birth, youth, maturity, old age, and death.

The other motto, equally pervasive in the alchemical literature, is *opus contra naturam*—"the work against nature." This image and motto seemingly contradicts the first one. It avers that in order to really wake up and become conscious we have to practice working with mindful intention against the inertial pull of the unconscious sleeplike habits of everyday life. Gurdjieff and other masters of the so-called Fourth Way, as well as some teachers in the Sufi, Zen, and Taoist lineages, are often identified with this way.

D. T. Suzuki (1980) wrote, "What is awakened in the Zen experience is not a 'new' experience but an 'old' one, which has been dormant since our loss of innocence. . . . The awakening is really the rediscovery or the excavation of a long-lost treasure . . . the finding ourselves back in our original abode where we lived even before our birth."

FOURTEEN

A MESSAGE OF SOLACE
FROM BEYOND

Susie, the two-year-old daughter of my niece Veronica, was playing in a small sidewalk park near a traffic intersection when she darted out into the street and was hit and killed by a slow-moving car. Her quick and sudden movements were witnessed by her four-year-old sister Jillian and by her horrified nanny Jaclyn, a twenty-seven-year-old first grade schoolteacher. The wheels of time for that family came to an abrupt halt at that moment and started again on a different cycle, with different momentum and with different, unforeseeable outcomes. Veronica, in shock, reached out to me by phone, knowing of the accidental death of my eight-year-old son Ari more than forty years before.

The loss of a beloved older family member is an occasion of grief and sorrow for which we learn to gradually prepare ourselves. The unexpected loss of a child in the beginning phase of life is a shock to all involved—for which no preparation is possible. Loving relatives and friends are stunned into uncomprehending silence, moving closer together to huddle at the edge of the abyss of the unknown. In my counseling practice, the personal experience of the loss of my child has provided me with the gift of empathic understanding in such situations. I am usually able to convey to the grieving survivors that healing is possible, though it may take a long time.

Author's note: I am grateful to my relatives Jon and Veronica Dreher for giving me permission to tell this story of after-death communication involving their daughter Susie.

189

My wife and daughter and I immediately made plans to fly to Washington State to support our beloved relatives and attend the memorial for Susie. The day before our departure, I had a body-therapy session that had been scheduled sometime previously. I had not shared the recent tragedy in my family with the therapist and did not expect or anticipate the following soul conversation that took place. While the therapist was working to release tension patterns along the left, receptive side of my back, I suddenly had a vision of a young girl, about seven or eight years old, whom I did not know or recognize, who was smiling at me. Wanting to dispel what I thought was a fleeting fantasy, I changed my focus of attention, but the vision of the young girl persisted. Her smile suggested that she knew me and wanted my attention. Then I got it—it was Susie, and she wanted to tell me something. There ensued the following telepathic dialogue.

First, I wanted to validate my recognition of who she was. Susie was two years old when she died, but this young girl appeared to be around seven or eight. (I should add here that I had met her only once in real life, when she was a baby in her mother's arms.) The answer to my unspoken question confirmed something I already knew—when we relate or communicate with an immortal soul, the being we perceive is ageless or in the prime of life. In the after-death realm, Susie was growing up fast, so to speak. In any case, her soul did not have the appearance of a two-year-old. I asked her to confirm what was happening, by showing me some of her possible future forms. I got brief flashes of her as a teenager and as an adult, but then the image settled back down to the seven- or eight-year-old form. The implied message was clear: as the young girl she would be able to articulate her thoughts more clearly than as the two-year-old, but the point of her visit was not to provide a preview of a possible future.

She wanted to say something important to her parents, through my channel—evidently cognizant of the fact that I was going to meet with them. That was also the reason for her happy smile—seemingly incongruous in the face of a tragic loss of life. It was the smile of recognition that told me that we knew each other, and it was also the smile of delight that a "live" contact was taking place. I got the sense, which I've also had on other occasions, that the souls of departed loved ones are constantly looking for opportunities to connect with their living relatives—whether directly, in dreams or visions, or indirectly, through mediums and psychics.

The receptiveness of the living is limited—primarily by false belief-systems that such communication is not possible, but also by the blocking of receptive sensitivity through the distractions of everyday life. In my case, I was in a relaxed, receptive mode as a result of the bodywork I was experiencing, and I was certainly aware of the upcoming family gathering. Hence Susie's evident delight: she had an important message for her parents and had found someone to deliver it.

A further important, perhaps the most important, factor that blocks the receptivity of the living to communication with departed souls is the traumatic shock of loss in the case of an accidental death. The trauma reaction involves a closing off to life and to connection through withdrawal and numbing. This explains why it frequently happens that a friend of the family, who is not so directly affected by the death, will be able to receive messages from the departed soul to pass on. This is what happened in my case. When my son Ari died, I did not have any direct communications or contacts with his soul for a very long time, though I believed in the possibility of such contact. A close friend, who was a gifted high-level sensitive, was able to relay messages from Ari to me. In fact, this is probably the most frequent request that professional psychics and mediums receive—to receive and send messages to departed loved ones. I sensed that this was one of the reasons for Susie's delight—she knew that direct communication with her parents would be difficult and unlikely, at least for a while.

Having established our soul connection and gotten my complete attention, here was the message the departed soul whose persona was named Susie wanted me to convey to her parents, smiling happily all the time and clearly growing up fast: "I'm okay, Mom and Dad, I'm fine. Don't blame yourselves—don't go into blame or guilt over what was done or not done. It's not your fault, not anybody's fault. I'm happy and free. I love you."

Susie's father Jon was working with police and lawyers to sort out vexing issues of legal responsibility and potential liability, in view of the fact that the driver of the vehicle was unlicensed and had a history of drug abuse. Both parents were also compassionately concerned for the potentially traumatic self-blame on the part of the nanny Jaclyn. Susie's message, conveyed calmly and with the wisdom of a mature soul, implied that conception and death, the entry into and departure from a particular life, are soul choices or matters of karma. These may not be known or understood by the persona until much later, perhaps not until after we have died ourselves. In any case, her essential message was that she was at peace and full of love and goodwill toward her relatives. She was definitely not "lost" and definitely not "gone."

In the ensuing dialogue between the "Susie" soul and me, it was sometimes hard to tell which messages were coming from her and what was coming from my own experience. One could say we were in agreement on the importance of distinguishing clearly between *grief* and *guilt*. Guilt and self-blame, though seemingly inevitable reactions, actually block the process of grieving. When my son Ari died in an accident in California, I was in New York—and yet I senselessly blamed myself for what I should have done or prevented or known. I was in a traumatic guilt reaction—trying to keep my emotions under control. What Susie and I both conveyed to her parents was the importance of releasing guilt or blame and instead permitting the grief, with all its tears and wailing. Grieving is immensely healing. Tears, we now know, contain serotonin, the calming, peace-inducing neurotransmitter.

People of Anglo-Saxon ancestry tend to keep the expression of emotions more under control, unlike Mediterranean and also many indigenous cultures. In the British Isles, the Irish have preserved the ancient custom of keening—or grief wailing. In some communities in former times, there were older women who could be engaged to provide keening at funeral ceremonies.

I suggested to Veronica and Jon that they find a peaceful, secluded place in nature where they could go, each one alone, and wail and howl their grief without reservations or shame. I told them how, when my son Ari died, I found a weeping willow tree, under whose canopy I could let the floodgates of grief open. For some, their grieving place might be the ocean, or the forest, or a quiet meadow. The essential point is to be alone in nature with your grief so that you are not concerned with other people's reactions.

I talked to Veronica and Jon about the importance of establishing or finding a support group with other parents who have prematurely lost a child, and I was glad to learn they had already done that. This was one difference, I realized, between the cultural environment in the early 1970s when my son died, and the present time. A child's death, in former times, created great isolation for the parents, because most of their acquaintances were unlikely to have a real sense of that blessedly uncommon experience. Now, with the proliferation of the internet, it is a relatively easy matter to find a small group of parents, in the same general locale, who also have had devastating experiences of this kind with their children. Such a group could also meet in person from time to time, and provide much-needed emotional support to one another.

From my experience counseling others who had lost a close family member, I also suggested that Veronica and Jon set aside one small area of a room in their house with a memorial altar space dedicated to their daughter. It could have a picture or two, fresh flowers or a plant, a candle that is lit at occasional meditative remembrance times. This could be especially valuable for their four-year-old, who might not get that much from the internet connection. It would be a tangible remembering place for her with her sister's spirit.

I urged Veronica and Jon above all to be considerate and gentle with each other, recognizing that the unspeakable trauma they shared might leave or reveal some raw emotional edges in their relationship. I knew from experience that some couples do not survive such a trauma. I was relieved to learn that they were already participating in grief-counseling sessions.

The final message that came through me from Susie's spirit to her parents was "I'm going to come back, if you want me and wish for it. In a couple of years, perhaps, and maybe as a boy next time." This last point seemed to reveal that soul's adventurous spirit—expressed also in her impulsive rushing out into the street. Veronica confirmed that she had sometimes had the intuitive flash that a boy was coming when she was first pregnant with Susie.

The message also confirmed for me, once again that, from the perspective of an immortal soul going through numerous incarnations in its journeys on planet Earth, death is literally not that big a deal—although, of course, for the families involved in a particular lifetime, it is the biggest deal of all.

At the memorial service for the family and friends I shared, with Jon and Veronica's permission, the essentials of the story of my connection with Susie's spirit. I also shared with them an exquisitely beautiful anonymous poem, called "Song of a Departed Child Spirit," which I had found many years before in some literature available at the Santo Domingo Pueblo, now called the Kewa Pueblo, in New Mexico.

Song of a Departed Child Spirit

I am on the way now,
traveling the road to where the spirits live,
the Spirit World.
I look at the road, far ahead, along that way.
Nothing bad happens to me, as I am a spirit.

I am a spirit, of course I am,
as I go on the fine clean road to the Spirit World.

My spirit meets the others, who have gone before me,
who are coming towards me.
I am glad to see them and be with them.
I know I have a right to be here now.

I must leave now because the Old Ones
have called me back.
I will go, I will obey their call.
There are places in the Spirit World
where all the people live whom you have known.
They have gone there, when their time came.

I cannot say what they will make of me.
I may take the form of a cloud.
I wish I could be a cloud.
I will take a chance on whatever is offered to me.
When a cloud comes this way, you may say,
"That is he!" or "There she is."

When I get to the place of spirits
I will hear whatever you ask.
You must always remember me.
When you talk about me,
in the Spirit World I can hear everything you say.

I am spirit now and I bless you.
I thank you for all you have done for me in past years.

I hope to see you some day.
We send you many good wishes, many good things.

Thank you.

GURDJIEFF AND THE GNOSTIC GOSPEL OF JUDAS

In 2006 there appeared the first English translation of a Gnostic text known as the Gospel of Judas. It had been lost for sixteen hundred years and was discovered in a cave in Egypt. Originally found in the 1970s, the manuscript was traded and moved across several continents, suffering major damage that reduced it to fragments. This fragmented text was finally translated by scholars from the original Coptic into English in 2001. The appearance of the text, and an article about it in *National Geographic* magazine (Lovgren 2006), caused a sensation, because it turned the traditional Christian conception of Judas as the prototypical traitor on its head. In this version of the story, Judas is portrayed as one of Jesus's closest disciples and friends, who carries out the so-called betrayal as a special assignment at Jesus's request and is rewarded by being given some secret, very high teachings that the other disciples did not get.

Although this picture of Judas as an especially favored and trusted disciple counters the generally accepted Gospel story of the archetypal traitor, there are some indications in the canonical Gospels that seem to suggest that Jesus anticipated, perhaps was even complicit in his own impending betrayal (Pagels and King 2007). One example is in the Gospel of John 13:27, when Jesus says to Judas, "Go and do quickly what you are going to do." This sounds almost as if there was some agreed-upon plan—and counters the familiar story that Judas "betrayed our Lord" for a measly thirty pieces of silver.

Students and readers of Gurdjieff's *All and Everything* no doubt recalled, as I did, that Gurdjieff had himself declared a similar perspective on the story of Judas—extremely divergent from that of the canonical Gospels. In Gurdjieff's account in *All and Everything,* Judas is called "not only the most faithful and devoted of all the near followers of Jesus Christ, but also, only thanks to his Reason and presence of mind, all the acts of this Sacred Individual (Jesus) could form that result . . . which . . . was . . . during twenty centuries the source of nourishment and inspiration for the majority of them in their desolate existence and made it at least a little endurable" (Gurdjieff 1950, 740).

G. I. Gurdjieff, who died in 1949, wrote *All and Everything* long before this Gospel of Judas, or any of the Gnostic texts known under the collective name of the Nag Hammadi library (after the cave in Egypt where they were found), had been rediscovered in the 1970s. The synchronicity confirms the notion that Gurdjieff was aware of and drew on secret texts and revelations that had been strenuously excised from orthodox teachings for two millennia—though they perhaps remained in certain secret societies.

As Elaine Pagels and Karen King point out in their study *Reading Judas* (2007), in the early centuries before the teachings we know today as Christianity were crystallized into the orthodoxy of the Catholic Church, there were numerous sects and groups scattered around the Mediterranean countries, with startlingly different versions of Christ's life and teaching and also having connections with esoteric Jewish and Gnostic teachings. There are mythic figures and references in the Gospel of Judas that would strike a modern Christian as bizarre in the extreme. At the same time, there are aspects of the teachings attributed to Jesus in this as in other Gnostic gospels that are in profound accord with a universal mystical vision.

I do not have the expertise to delve into the particularities of Gnostic doctrines in the Gospel of Judas, although I was struck by the fact that the text, no doubt because of its fragmented condition, gives a very inadequate and obviously incomplete account of the *reasons* for

Judas's betrayal. It does make clear that Judas goes on a particular mission at the explicit request of the Master—even although this mission ends with Jesus's death. It quotes Jesus as prophesying that "You will be the thirteenth, and you will be cursed by the other generations . . . but you will exceed all of them" (Kasser et al. 2006, 2–33).

Gurdjieff's comments on this story make the curse and the evil reputation of Judas's name understandable. According to this Gnostic gospel fragment, Judas is actually regarded by Jesus as exceptionally devoted and faithful. He is given a special and difficult assignment for which Jesus rewards him by giving him secret teachings in a vision—which the other disciples don't receive. Judas is given this special reward because he will miss the ceremony of the Last Supper in which all the other disciples are going to participate.

The text of the Gospel of Judas relates how in his vision Judas saw "a great and magnificent house with many people." Jesus tells him that this was not a house that mortal men could enter, but rather the "eternal realm with the holy angels." Jesus then proceeds to take Judas aside and relates to him cosmic secrets about a "great and boundless realm . . . in which there is a great invisible Spirit." Other passages, tantalizingly incomplete, speak of high angelic realms, filled with luminaries and immortal *aeons* engaged in creating and guiding humanity and the cosmos. Jesus, still addressing Judas, concludes, "Look, you have been told everything. Lift up your eyes and look at the cloud and the light within it and the stars surrounding it. The star that leads the way is your star" (Kasser et al. 2006, 44). Then there are a couple of sentences simply stating that Judas met some priests and handed Jesus over to them.

Although the traditional story that Judas betrayed Jesus for a bribe of "thirty pieces of silver" from the soldiers coming to capture Jesus is not in this account, what is still missing in the Gospel of Judas is any explanation of *why* Jesus asked him to do it as a special favor. Perhaps this is missing due to the fragmentary nature of the surviving text. Nor do the modern writers have any answer to this obvious question. Thus Rodolphe Kasser, in his commentary, says that "Judas. . . performs the greatest service for Jesus . . . handing him over to be executed so that the divine being within Jesus can escape the trappings of his material body" (Kasser et al. 2006, 91).

But this makes no sense: Why would a divine being like Jesus need to have a human associate bring him to the arrest and execution for which he knew he was already targeted? As Pagels and King point out, the other Gospel narrators tell the accepted story, but never really address the vexing question of why Judas did this, or of why Jesus apparently foresaw his arrest and acquiesced in it. He says to Judas, as he is leaving, "Do quickly what you are going to do" (John 13:27). Judas arrives with the soldiers, Jesus asks them who they are looking for and identifies himself as Jesus, and the soldiers "fall to the ground" in shock. He tells them again who he is, and tells them to let go of another man they are holding. According to this account, Jesus was in charge of the whole arrest scenario. It had all been foreordained (Pagels and King 2007).

That he is asking Judas a special favor is implied by the fact that Jesus prophesies that Judas will be cursed forever and so rewards him with a magnificent cosmological vision. Jesus foresaw and predicted that he was about to be arrested and killed. With his superior transcendent perception, he must have known that the priests and guards knew what he was doing and were coming to arrest him. Why was Judas sent on this apparently unnecessary and accursed mission to guide the soldiers to his teacher? Clearly it was an assigned task of great importance, for which Judas received a supreme reward of beatific cosmic visions. The notion that Judas betrayed the Master for the infamous thirty pieces of silver is not mentioned in the Judas gospel at all—this was clearly inserted into the Gospel of Matthew to provide some kind of base motivation for the allegedly treacherous Judas (Matthew 26:13).

I believe Gurdjieff's version of this story provides the missing element of the *reason why* Judas was asked by Jesus to perform this mission—a mission that cost Judas his life and his reputation forever. In Gurdjieff's version, as related by his alter ego Beelzebub in *All and*

Everything, the basic reason for Judas's mission of apparent betrayal was to buy some time for Jesus to carry out the ritual of the Last Supper with the other disciples.

I must . . . inform you that when this Sacred Individual Jesus Christ, intentionally actualized from Above in a planetary body of a terrestrial being, completely formed Himself for a corresponding existence, He decided to actualize the mission imposed on Him from Above, through the way of enlightening the reason of these terrestrial three-brained beings, by means of twelve different types of beings, chosen from among them and who were specially enlightened and prepared by him personally.

And so, in the very heat of His Divine Activities, surrounding circumstances independent of Him were so arranged, that not having carried out His intention, i.e., not having had time to explain certain truths and to give the required instructions for the future, He was compelled to allow the premature cessation of his planetary existence to be accomplished.

He then decided, together with these twelve terrestrial beings intentionally initiated by Him, to have recourse to the sacred sacrament Almznoshinoo—the process of the actualization of which sacred sacrament was already well known to all of them, as they had already acquired in their presences all the data for its fulfillment—so that He should have the possibility, while He still remained in such a cosmic individual state, to finish the preparation begun by Him for the fulfillment of the plan designed for actualization of the mission imposed on Him from Above.

And so . . . when having decided on this and being ready to begin with the preliminary preparations required for this sacred sacrament, it then became clear that it was utterly impossible to do this, as it was too late; they were all surrounded by beings, called "guards" and their arrest and everything that would follow from it, was expected at any moment. . . .

This wise, onerous and disinterestedly devoted manifestation taken upon himself consisted in this, that while in a state of desperation on ascertaining that it was impossible to fulfill the required preliminary procedure for the actualization of the sacred Almznoshinoo, this Judas, now a Saint, leaped from his place and hurriedly said:

"I shall go and do everything in such a way that you should have the possibility of fulfilling this sacred preparation without hindrance, and meanwhile set to work at once."

Having said this, he approached Jesus Christ and having confidentially spoken with Him a little and received His blessing, hurriedly left.

The others, indeed without hindrance finished everything necessary for the possibility of accomplishing this sacred process Almznoshinoo. (Gurdjieff 1950, 740–2)

As so often in Gurdjieff's published writings, he does not expand on the "sacred process Almznoshinoo," leaving the deeper layers of meaning for readers to ascertain for themselves. Nevertheless, according to this reading of the story, Jesus needed time to carry out the central Christian rite of Holy Communion, in other words the original "Last Supper." Here is what the contemporary online information source Wikipedia says about the origin of this rite, known as the Eucharist.

The **Eucharist,** also called **Holy Communion,** the **Lord's Supper,** is a rite considered by most Christian churches to be a sacrament. According to some *New Testament* books, it was instituted by Jesus Christ during his Last Supper. Giving his disciples bread and wine during the Passover meal, Jesus commanded his followers to "do this in memory of me," while referring to the bread as "my body" and the wine as "my blood." Through the Eucharistic celebration Christians remember Christ's sacrifice of himself once and for all on the cross.

Christians generally recognize a special presence of Christ in this rite, though they differ about exactly how, where, and when Christ is present. While all agree that there is no perceptible change in the elements, some believe that they actually become the body and blood of Christ, others believe the true Body and Blood of Christ are really present in, with and under the bread and wine (whose reality remains unchanged), others believe in a "real" but merely spiritual presence of Christ in the Eucharist, and still others take the act to be only a symbolic reenactment of the Last Supper. (emphasis in the original)

I will leave it to the reader to ponder whether and how Gurdjieff's story of the events surrounding the original Last Supper affects their understanding and their beliefs about this central Christian rite.

In *All and Everything,* almost as an afterthought, Gurdjieff, speaking in the persona of Beelzebub, sarcastically suggests that the reason that the compilers of Holy Writ allowed such a profound misrepresentation of the character of Judas to come into the Gospels is that they wanted to somehow belittle the significance of Jesus Christ himself. "He appeared to be so naïve, so unable to feel and see beforehand, in a word, so unperfected that in spite of knowing and existing together with this Judas so long, He failed to sense and be aware that this immediate disciple of His was such a perfidious traitor and that he would sell Him for thirty worthless pieces of silver" (Gurdjieff 1950, 742).

We see from this version of the Judas story, that Gurdjieff's reading of this, as of other religious myths, opens up much deeper layers of significance and meanings in well-known but often misunderstood stories. The publication of the Gnostic Gospel of Judas, two thousand years after the historical events related, provides us with an unexpected confirmation of his unusually penetrating and insightful perspectives.

REFERENCES

Adamson, Sophia. 2012. *Through the Gateway of the Heart.* 2nd ed. Petaluma, CA: Solarium Press.

Amaringo, Pablo, and Luis Eduardo Luna. 1991. *Ayahuasca Visions: The Religious Iconography of a Peruvian Shaman.* Berkeley, CA: North Atlantic Books.

Badiner, Allan. 2015. *Zig Zag Zen: Buddhism and Psychedelics.* Santa Fe, NM: Synergetic Press.

Bedi, Gillinder, David Hyman, and Harriet de Wit. 2010. "Is Ecstasy an 'Empathogen'? Effects of Methylenedioxyamphetamine on Prosocial Feelings and Identification of Emotional States in Others." *Biological Psychiatry* 68:1134–40.

Bedi, Gillinder, K. Luan Phan, and Mike Angstadt. 2009. "Effects of MDMA on Sociability and Neural Response to Social Threat and Social Reward." *Psychopharmacology* 207:73–83.

Dass, Ram, Ralph Metzner, and Gary Bravo. 2010. *Birth of a Psychedelic Culture.* Santa Fe, NM: Synergetic Press.

Douvris, George. 2016. *Crossing More Karma Zones: The Family Odyssey.* Self-published.

Ellis, Ed, and Ralph Metzner. 2011. "From Traumatized Vet to Peacemaker Activist." *MAPS Bulletin* 21, no. 1: 9–10.

Foster, Steven, and Meredith Little. 1989. *The Roaring of the Sacred River.* New York: Prentice Hall.

Gleason, Judith. 1992. *Oya: In Praise of an African Goddess.* New York: HarperCollins. Originally published in 1987.

Gurdjieff, G. I. 1950. *All and Everything: Beelzebub's Tales to his Grandson.* New York: E. P. Dutton.

———. 1963. *Meetings with Remarkable Men.* New York: E. P. Dutton.

Hagenbach, Dieter, and Lucius Werthmüller. 2013. *Mystic Chemist: The Life of Albert Hofmann and His Discovery of LSD.* Santa Fe, NM: Synergetic Press.

Hofmann, Albert. 1979. *LSD: Mein Sorgenkind.* Stuttgart, Germany: Klett-Cotta.

———. 2011. *Tun und Lassen: Essays, Gedanken, und Gedichte.* Solothurn, Switzerland: Nachtschatten Verlag.

Kalff, Dora. 2004. *Sandplay: A Psychotherapeutic Approach to the Psyche.* Cloverdale, CA: Temenos Press.

Kasser, Rodolphe, Marvin Meyer, and Gregor Wurst, eds. 2006. *The Gospel of Judas.* New York: National Geographic.

Levine, Peter A. 2010. *In an Unspoken Voice.* Berkeley, CA: North Atlantic Books.

Lovgren, Stefan. 2006. "Lost Gospel Revealed; Says Jesus Asked Judas to Betray Him." *National Geographic News* April 6.

Mack, John E. 1991. *Passport to the Cosmos: Human Transformation and Alien Encounters.* New York: Crown.

———. 1994. *Abduction: Human Encounters with Aliens.* New York: Charles Scribner's Sons.

Mays, Buddy. *Indian Villages of the Southwest.* San Francisco: Chronicle Books, 1985.

McIntyre, Joan. 1974. *Mind in the Waters.* New York: Scribner's.

McKenna, Dennis. 2012. *The Brotherhood of the Screaming Abyss: My Life with Terence McKenna.* Saint Cloud, MN: North Star Press.

McKenna, Terence. 1991. *The Archaic Revival.* San Francisco: HarperSanFrancisco.

———. 1992. *Food of the Gods: The Search for the Original Tree of Knowledge.* New York: Bantam.

McKenna, Terence, and Dennis McKenna. 1975. *The Invisible Landscape.* New York: Seabury Press.

Meech, Richard. 2009. *Vine of the Soul: Encounters with Ayahuasca.* www.vineofthesoul.com. DVD.

Metzner, Ralph. 1968. "On the Evolutionary Significance of Psychedelics." *Main Currents in Modern Thought* 25:1 (Sept.–Oct.), 20–5.

———. 1971. *Maps of Consciousness.* New York: Macmillan.

———. 1999. *Green Psychology: Transforming Our Relationship to the Earth.* Rochester, VT: Park Street Press.

———. 2013. *The Toad and the Jaguar: A Field Report of Underground Research on a Visionary Medicine.* Berkeley, CA: Regent Press.

———, ed. 2014. *The Ayahuasca Experience: A Sourcebook on the Sacred Vine of Spirits.* Rochester, VT: Park Street Press.

———. 2015. *Allies for Awakening.* Berkeley, CA: Regent Press.

———. 2017. *Ecology of Consciousness.* Oakland, CA: Reveal Press/New Harbinger Publications.

Naranjo, Claudio. 1973. *The Healing Journey.* New York: Ballantine.

Nichols, David, et al. 1997. "The Great Entactogen-Empathogen Debate." *MAPS Bulletin* 4:2.

Oss, O. T., and O. N. Oeric. 1976. *Psilocybin: Magic Mushroom Grower's Guide.* Berkeley, CA: Lux Natura.

Pagels, Elaine, and Karen L. King. 2007. *Reading Judas: The Gospel of Judas and the Shaping of Christianity.* New York: Viking Penguin.

Passie, Torsten. 2012. *Healing with Entactogens.* Foreword by Ralph Metzner. Santa Cruz, CA: MAPS.

Passie, Torsten, et al. 2005. "Ecstasy (MDMA) Mimics the Post-orgasmic State: Impairment of Sexual Drive and Function during Acute MDMA Effects May Be Due to Increased Prolactin Secretion." *Medical Hypotheses* 64: 899–903.

Rothenberg, David. 2008. *Thousand Mile Song: Whale Music in a Sea of Sound.* New York: Basic Books/Perseus Books. Includes CD combining music with whale sounds.

Shulgin, Alexander. N.d. "Surfing the Rave: Ecstacy [*sic*]; Interview with Dr. Alexander Shulgin." www.mdma.net/alexander-shulgin/mdma.html. Accessed May 8, 2018.

Shulgin, Alexander, and Ann Shulgin. 1991. *PIHKAL: A Chemical Love Story.* Berkeley, CA: Transform Press.

———. 1997. *TIHKAL: The Continuation.* Berkeley, CA: Transform Press.

Slomoff, Danny. 1986. "Ecstatic Spirits: A West African Healer at Work." *Shaman's Drum,* summer, 27–31.

Stolaroff, Myron J. 2004. *The Secret Chief Revealed.* Santa Cruz, CA: MAPS. An earlier version of this essay and correspondence was published in the *MAPS Bulletin* 21:1 (2011).

Suzuki, D. T. 1980. "The Awakening of a New Consciousness in Zen." In Joseph Campbell, ed. *Man and Transformation: Papers from the Eranos Yearbooks,* vol. 2. Princeton, NJ: Princeton University Press, 179–85.

Van Dusen, Wilson. 1979. *The Natural Depth in Man.* New York: Swedenborg Foundation.

———. 2004. *The Presence of Other Worlds.* Great Barrington, MA: Steiner Books. First published in 1974.

Weyler, Rex. 1986. *Song of the Whale.* Garden City, NY: Doubleday/Anchor.

Whitten, Norman. 1985. *Sicuanga Runa.* Champaign: University of Illinois Press.

INDEX